Poems Across The Big Sky:

An Anthology of Montana Poets

Many Voices Press
Flathead Valley Community College

Softbound
ISBN – 978-09795185-0-8 (alk. paper)
ISBN – 0-9795185-0-4 (alk. paper)

© 2007 Many Voices Press

For more information on our books, write Many Voices Press,
Flathead Valley Community College, 777 Grandview Drive
Kalispell, Montana 59901
(406) 756-3822
www.fvcc.edu

Cataloging-in-Publication data on file at the Library of Congress.
Library of Congress Control Number 2007903634

Created, produced, and designed in the United States.
Printed in the United States.

Poems Across the Big Sky

Board of Editors:

Sandra Alcosser
Tami Haaland
Greg Keeler
Rick Newby
Mandy Smoker

Roger Dunsmore
Lowell Jaeger
Ed Lahey
Sheryl Noethe
Paul Zarzyski

Cover painting by Jennifer Fallein

Cover design by Sally Johnson

Special thanks to Elizabeth Dear, Margaret Kingsland, Kathy Hughes, Danette Lale, Hannah Bissell, Sally Johnson, Jennifer Fallein, Amy Jaeger, Mandy Smoker, Krys Holmes, Mark Gibbons, Lois Red Elk, Minerva Allen, Vic Charlo, April Charlo, Sophie Mays, the Native American Language Teacher Training Institute, Montana Arts Council, Montana Committee for the Humanities, and so many others who helped in so many ways.

Many Voices Press is a non-profit literary press from Flathead Valley Community College. We depend on the generosity of people like you. Please send your tax-deductible contributions to:

Many Voices Press
Lowell Jaeger, Editor
777 Grandview Drive
Kalispell, Montana 59901
(406) 756-3822

Contents:

Introduction: "All This Wild Beauty"

A year before the state's 1989 centennial, Montanans were delighted and stunned by the publication of an 1158-page anthology of Montana literature, *The Last Best Place*. Edited by William Kittredge and Annick Smith, it was the first anthology of Montana writing which had been attempted since Joseph Kinsey Howard's 1946 *Montana Margins: A State Anthology*. It immediately generated praise, as well as controversy— praise for its ambition, controversy over who and what had been left out. Over the past twenty years other writers and editors have stepped forward with additional collections of literature from Montana. These include *Writing Montana: Literature Under the Big Sky*, edited by Rick Newby and Suzanne Hunger (1996); *The Best of Montana's Short Fiction*, edited by William Kittredge and Allen Morris Jones (2004); and *Montana Women Writers: A Geography of the Heart*, edited by Caroline Patterson (2006); to name a few. What has been missing is an anthology of contemporary Montana poetry. Now, thanks to the inspiration and work of Lowell Jaeger, with the assistance of nine other poet-editors across the state, Montanans will be able to savor an important new anthology, *Poems Across the Big Sky*.

Not surprisingly, Jaeger himself and some of the associate editors are poets who are also faculty members from Montana colleges or universities. Many of the writers represented in this collection are writers who have passed through their classrooms, been hosted by their campuses or communities, and featured in local, regional, or state-wide book festivals. This book began with Lowell Jaeger's determination to honor the voices of former students whose papers had been entrusted to him, and to bring forward the work of writers who may not have as wide an audience as they deserve. Thanks to Lowell Jaeger and to Montana poets Sandra Alcosser, Roger Dunsmore, Tami Haaland, Greg Keeler, Ed Lahey, Rick Newby, Sheryl Noethe, M.L. Smoker, and Paul Zarzyski for helping to identify a new generation of Montana poets to celebrate. Woven through each section are also some examples of the work of widely-known writers such as Richard Hugo, James Welch, Madeline DeFrees, Robert Pack, John Haines, James Harrison, Patricia Goedicke, and others who need no introduction. Sadly, equally important Montana poets such as Patrick Todd are not represented, nor do we have Gary Holthaus, Leonard Wallace Robinson, Denice Scanlon, Roberta Hill Whiteman, to name a few. But this collection was not intended to be a comprehensive or an historical survey of Montana poetry. That challenge awaits another editorial board and another anthology.

Whether in Montana classrooms or in solitude, the beauty, complexity, and struggle of lives in Montana have inspired the remarkable variety of voices which comprise *Poems Across the Big Sky*. In "The Lost Meadow" Aunda Cole, one of Jaeger's late students, writes of "All this wild beauty." She is referring to a high mountain meadow, now turning to forest, but her line can serve as well to describe this unexpected poetry collection. Startling, thrilling, shocking, and transporting works are gathered here, a record of Montanans' sensibilities at the end of the twentieth century and the beginning of the twenty-first. The poets included are female as well as male, Native American as well as non-Native, gay as well as straight, urban as well as rural. Some of them write in the Native languages of Montana, and also in English. Together they provide a portrait of Montana which challenges and prods us to a new, more inclusive and comprehensive understanding of the bittersweet essence of contemporary life in Montana Reservations, cities, small towns, isolated ranches, cabins, prairies, and mountains.

In a very real sense we Montanans are all living in Indian Country, as John Haines reminds us with "The Eye in the Rock." One of the most important contributions to our understanding of Montana literature is the variety of tribal voices gathered in this anthology. The cultural erasure of the Native American languages, histories, and tribal experiences of Montana is challenged again and again in *Poems Across the Big Sky*. Its poems employing the Cheyenne, Salish, Lakota, and Assiniboine languages are an important contribution to a larger understanding of the Montana experience. The need to reclaim what's been forgotten, and to re-inscribe it on the reader's consciousness is evident in the first bilingual work in this collection, Heather Cahoon's Salish-titled poem which opens: "Dixon wasn't always known for its only bar./It was a place the Pend d' Oreille/would go for plums. In its name/its purpose, *plums at junction of two rivers*." With its nod to James Welch and Richard Hugo in the opening line, it announces and it claims a new/old way of understanding where we are in space and time.

Thanks to Victor Charlo, Richard Littlebear, M.L. Smoker, Henry Real Bird, Minerva Allen and other poets from Montana tribes we can see words from some of the ancient languages of this part of the continent here on the page. Even though most readers will not know how to pronounce them, we can rejoice that there are people on this earth who do, and who still speak and sing such words. We can be grateful that there are Native Montanans who have generously written them down, translated them, and shared them with us all. We can hope that one day we will have the privilege of hearing these poets read their poems, using two languages, and helping others to appreciate the forms, sounds, and rhythms of the languages of their tribes. Seeing Salish on the page we can empathize with Victor Charlo in "Agnes" when he remembers her Salish language lesson and asks, "Why did I learn how to write? Why did I want to?/Is it worth the loss of your world going away?" With Minerva Allen and M. L. Smoker we can savor intimate domestic moments on the bridge between two worlds: the ancient tribal world and that of the twenty-first century.

Poems Across the Big Sky brings us many poems reminding us of Montana's rural as well as tribal roots. In Richard Hugo's "Driving Montana," which leaps off the last pages of the book to remind us of his mastery, and his advice to "write about what you know," the richness of Montana's open spaces and its small towns contrasts with contemporary poems such as Shirley Steele's "Monuments," where truck bodies rusting into the landscape memorialize an agricultural world of farms and "small, warm western towns/that somehow died." For Dave Waldman "Cars in the River" are monuments of our mortality too, reminders of "how these armored road-warriors/too shall pass. Like us...." Playing with the trout fishing meditations beloved of Montana writers, including Hugo, with tongue in cheek he notices how "Now a fat dark Merc cools/in the shady flow, submerged to the dash...." In 2007 Montana writers are able to celebrate their mentors, including Hugo and Welch, and carry forward their legacy with a kind of jaunty confidence.

The editors have also gathered a number of poems which bring fresh attention to the fact that at this point in time the vast majority of Montanans live in small cities, not on farms or ranches. Foremost, of course, are Ed Lahey's Butte poems, and it is wonderful to find more than one here. John Holbrook's "The Weightless Spray of a Perfect Dive" springs from a bridge in Missoula into a meditation on youth, beauty, choice, transience. In Phil Cohea's "Walking Helena with Nick" we find a poet's thoughts on history, architecture, mathematics, relationship, the Universe in a small Montana city. Tami Haaland's beautiful poems bring us the rimrocks of Billings in "Let Deer Come Crashing," and the downtown Billings surprise of the poem "Kathy Catches a Train," while Franco Littlelight shares Billings and classic Indian humor and pity for human frailty in "Montana Avenue." Without taking the state's natural beauty for granted, contemporary Montana writers move more fluidly between the natural and human-made worlds presently found in Montana than did many of their predecessors.

There is an assumption of the loss of innocence in Montana now, and it makes irony, cynicism, humor, rage, and a modified kind of humility possible in contemporary poems from Montana. It makes for very few poems of romantic love, though it gives us more poems of the complex challenges of long-time love, and ruminations on the love of children, the complicated love of parents, of place. Philip Burgess' "Gypsy Son" comes to mind, as do Lowell Jaeger's "Learning to Dance," Jennifer Fallein's "Irises", Jennifer Kreiss' "Wives' Tale", Rick Newby's "Night Vigil," Mac Swan's "Pruning," Greg Keeler's "Philipsburg '94", (so near yet far from Hugo's "degrees of gray" in the same small town); and Tom Elliott's ferociously beautiful "Mother." The poems in this anthology do not claim to come from the last best place. Tami Haaland's deer crashing in the brush on the rimrocks above Billings are being chased by a woman and barking dog. They struggle to survive in the urban/wildland intersection of contemporary Montana, even as the poet does, "City on one side, sage and sandstone above,...."

Often, "All this wild beauty" belongs to the human heart of Montana. Accordingly, there are many poems here which shock and startle the reader: Brenda Nesbitt's "Loki/The Messenger" with its meditation on the injured turtle with its cracked shell and beating heart, and its message to her:

> ....That my shell
> Is cracked. My heart exposed.
> My heart beating.
> How I've outgrown
> this self-imposed, limitation
> of form.

The late Irvin Moen's "Cuffs" is another, a beautifully constructed meditation on madness and justice, "the State's right to refuse/my right to die." In this poem, as in Casey Charles' "Pony, Montana", the big skies, the landscape, the small towns no longer represent either escape or solace. Dread, fear, and desperation, too, are found under the big sky and in the small towns of Montana. For Moen,

> Fragmented ranches
> and towns
> reel me closer
> to the State Hospital. It lurks
> just beyond the carved leap
> of the horizon.

We are in a very different world and time now, and it is no longer so "high, wide, and handsome" as Joseph Kinsey Howard's Montana, nor so easy to embrace as "the last best place." The poems of this anthology record a different time in Montana's history. With Paul Zarzyski's "The Day the War Began", Dennie Carpenter's "What Makes a Patriot?" Jim Soular's "Tripwire", Jennifer Greene's "Robbed", and Judy Blunt's "Making Peace" we see how the global conflicts in the world outside Montana are brought home to the wide skies of our state: how they intrude on our consciousness, distract us from the beauty of the sky and prairie and mountains, demand that we participate in a wider world. Trapped like Zarzyski's mouse in the slick tin feeder into which he tips grain for horses, we make the best we can of our present moment. Sometimes, like the mouse, we get lucky. In those times we celebrate.

This new anthology is cause for celebration. We can support its many voices, and Montana's creative inspiration by preserving and protecting the land, buying more books of poetry, subscribing to more poetry magazines, organizing and attending more readings and book festivals, and continuing to support schools and systems of higher education which teach, host, and honor creativity and community in all of their forms in this new century.

Margaret C. Kingsland
Missoula, Montana
May, 2007

Editor's Notes: How This Anthology Came to Be

A plane arcs across the night sky, and I'm peering down on the vastness below. I'm unsettled by the number of yardlights in the middle of nowhere. People live down there? I try to calculate how far they must commute for groceries in Helena, Missoula, Great Falls. I strain to imagine their lives centered around livestock and crops. Kids who ride a yellow bus to school. Dogs barking after the mail carrier. The dust that rises and settles along the gravel, marking a passing car. Now and again a stranger, maybe lost, turns in the drive and knocks uncertainly to ask for directions. Even out here the world comes knocking. Or someone's spying on you from his window seat, jetting overhead. I mark how the darkness of uninhabited space gets broken up with the clustered glow of streetlamps from the next little town, the next little town, the next little town. So much space between us.

I fly home near midnight into the Flathead Valley, end of the road for the flight crew who know the routine—taxi to the motel and back to the airport at dawn to ferry people to bigger places like Salt Lake or Seattle. "Where are you headed?" asks my seatmate, and when I say I live here, he looks puzzled. "What do you do?" he asks, meaning how on earth do you scratch out a living in territory where mostly people drive through and buy postcards. He wants to hear that I raise horses, which I've tried and failed. Or I'm a backcountry guide. Or maybe I'm just kidding, and I'm visiting from Columbus, Ohio. He doesn't want to hear that I teach at a community college, so I seldom bother with that. I wouldn't dream of telling him I'm a poet; might as well unzip my face and reveal my hideous alien third eye.

Then, too, the locals look a bit sideways at poets. I was sitting in a bar when I first moved to Montana, endeavoring to strike up a conversation with a guy and his wife on the barstools beside me. We had to shout above the band. I told them I teach at the community college. When they asked what I taught, instead of saying I teach English—which is a likely conversation-stopper on its own—I was liquor-loosened enough to blurt out the unholy word . . . poetry. The band went quiet, not because of me, but I was sorry I'd said what I said. Both of them looked away and nursed a few sips from their mugs. Eventually, the wife turned to me, screwed up her face curiously, and asked, "What's there to teach about chickens?"

That same year I read my poems at the county library. The well-meaning librarian gushed over my introduction and called me a "famous poet." An old ranchhand slouched in the back row, squinting when I read, like I'd caused him pain. He came up to me afterwards and shook my hand. "Must be tough," he said, shifting a wad of chew from one cheek to another, " . . . being so famous . . . when nobody ever heard of you." Which brings this to mind: one of my favorite Montana poets once complained to me, "I could drop my books from an airplane, and people wouldn't stoop to pick them up." He shall remain nameless. Mostly, all Montana poets are nameless to most other Montanans.

In the United States of America, it's tough being a poet. NASCAR pit crew guys are better known and better-paid. So is almost everyone else. But here in Montana, maybe it's especially tough for poets because we are disconnected from the thin network of poetry publishers and promoters, most of whom are walled up in urban centers. All around us, here under the Big Sky, are millions of acres of national forests and wilderness areas, and precious few venues for poems. I hear talk about what a swell place Montana is for writers and artists, and sometimes at an out-of-state conference, people who should know better talk about my home state as if I reside elbow-to-elbow with fellow poets. It's true; there are a lot of poets here. But it's also true we hardly know one another. Sure, part of the problem is that we are separated by rugged landscape. From Chicago, you can drive to St. Louis, Minneapolis, Detroit, or Des Moines in less time than it takes me to motor from my house to Billings. But the harder part may be that we savor a generous share of solitude, and this place surely comes well-supplied with that.

The pilot says it's time to fasten our seatbelts, prepare for our landing. We've just crested the Swan Range, and I'm looking down on the beautiful Flathead Valley. I shake my head. So many yardlights in every direction. From the air at night, my home turf looks like it could be the dense suburbs of Seattle. But no, it's each of us on his own couple of acres, keeping the trees between us, imagining we live hidden away on the frontier. I and so many Montanans hold tight to our right to be left alone. We've earned what we came here for. We hardly know our neighbors' names. Daily we pay the price.

One late afternoon after teaching freshman comp and creative writing at Flathead Valley Community College for nearly twenty-five years—fifteen credits a semester for fifty semesters!—I hunched blurry-eyed under the lamp, scratching red ink on student essays. I stretched back in my chair, took a deep breath, closed my eyes, and kicked lightly under my desk, the toe of my boot tapping a slow rhythm against three cardboard boxes that had been haunting me for years. I'd inherited, one by one, the life's work of three poets. Three of my best students. Now dead and gone. Hundreds of poems in each box, entrusted to me by relatives who had no clue where else to go with all these strange scribblings left behind.

I had no clue where to go with them either. Seemed like a terrible sadness I pushed here and piled there until they came to rest at my feet, and I tried to forget. Now, leaning back in my chair, I thought about what would happen to each of these boxes if I slid on the ice and drove off a cliff into the lake on my way home. The janitors would likely stack them on a dolly and wheel them to the dumpsters. I looked at my own poems tacked to the walls, and stared at rows of file folders and notebooks. My life's work. Enough paper for a fourth box under the desk. A short span of days after they fished me out of the frigid waters, the same conscientious cleaner-uppers would unceremoniously dispose of all my words in the same dumpster. Ashes to ashes, etc. This valley in winter can stay overcast for weeks. There's good reason my neighbors flee southward when the winds turn cold. I wasn't having a pleasant afternoon.

Here is the history of how this anthology came to light. I've thought about not telling the truth, because I know skeptics will snicker at what I'm about to say. I didn't want my three dead friends to suffer that sort of mockery. Still, to be silent with what I have to tell is too much compromise, another sort of mockery. The idea for this anthology came to me in a dream. There, I've said it. I went to bed thinking about those three archived lives entrusted to me and fell asleep feeling a bit hopeless. I had a very powerful dream. The kind you wake up and you can't remember details, but you feel in your gut something important happened during the night. I dreamt of my three poets. I don't know how events of the dream transpired, but I know we talked, and when my alarm went off that morning, I felt resolved. I knew what I had to do.

Individual poets win awards and grants and acclamations of one sort or another. Good for them. They get their photos in *Poets and Writers*. They book reading tours and soon lapse into obscurity. The world says, "So what?" And I can't argue with that; think of all the difficulties this planet has to endure. In Africa, child soldiers die under the command of rebel madmen. In the Middle East, the God of Abraham tears at his chin whiskers to witness horrors committed, one believer against another. Here in Montana Indian youths prostitute themselves to feed meth addictions. Hail ruins a wheat harvest, diseases kill a herd of cattle, banks foreclose, and families are forced off the land of their pioneering ancestors. For that matter, the Weather Channel warns me The Yellowstone Caldera—hotspot of the earth's thermal rumblings—is likely to blow, and when it does, we can all kiss our sweet collective behinds a final goodbye. Then someone sees me on the street or in a restaurant and mentions he's read a poem of mine, and I feel glad, but at the same time I'm filled with wonder to imagine my words having occupied someone else's body, if only for the time it takes to brush his teeth. Yes, I could have made books from my dead poets' archives, finagled them into print, so they would have their fifteen minutes of public notice; then their works would die like they did—too soon. Or I could drop their poems from an airplane, and no one would stoop to pick them up. I wanted to give my friends better than that.

I wanted to give them community. I wanted to bind their lonely, separate writing lives with others who are writers and who feel alone. My three dead friends knew the wisdom in that. It was their idea. They wanted to join their words in a collection of voices that reached out across the Big Sky, over the wide open spaces between us. These three deceased poets, from their vantage point in the stars, looked down on the twinkle of yardlights peppered in the darkness, and they heard a hundred pens on the pages of a hundred notebooks, scratching out the small truths of daily life in a gorgeous and difficult place. And they didn't want those voices and notebooks to end up in the dumpster, either.

From the start, this anthology was an exercise in democracy. I learned a lot about democracy. Democracy requires faith in the good judgment of others. Democracy says two heads are better than one, and—even as crazy and confused as the whole process gets—more heads are better still. Charged with purpose the morning I awoke from my dream, I phoned nine other prominent Montana poets, enlisted them onto a board of editors, and offered them a rough sketch of *Poems Across the Big Sky*. Each of us would choose nine additional poets from our circle of acquaintances, with emphasis on former students and community poets who hadn't been given the recognition their talents deserved. "You choose your poets," I said, "and you choose the poems."

It was an easy sell. Nine phone calls on a wet February morning in 2006, and ten Montana poets pulled together as a board of editors. I knew the names of these other nine; maybe I'd met most of them. Were we close associates? Could we be called friends? No. But it was the beginning of community, and I felt something like my dad must have felt as a union organizer in the lumber mills across Wisconsin. Or maybe, together, we were something like the scattered communities of the Montana Territory, learning how to share resources, how to speak in a collective voice, aiming for statehood. Too grandiose, I know. But it felt good. Felt right. And I was proud to introduce my three—Brenda Nesbitt, Irvin Moen, and Aunda Cole—and several others into the community of Montana writers.

Here's a thumbnail portrait of the spirits driving this project from the get-go:

Brenda Nesbitt came dancing (literally) into my classroom in the late 80s before my college owned a campus. Flathead Valley Community College was a rag-tag collection of rented storefronts, an abandoned car dealership, and a three-story defunct YMCA, the top floor of which had been condemned and boarded up against occupancy. I'd seen Brenda crossing the street from classroom to classroom, her long hair a wild array of braids and ribbons and dandelions, her slight form floating beneath wispy ankle-length skirts and brightly embroidered blouses. Looked like Woodstock had found its way to town, especially her euphoric, ever-smiling face, and her spontaneous leaps and twirls out of nowhere, as if she moved to a music all her own. And with that same rainbow on her face, she read her poems in class, tales of startling pain–abusive father, hillbilly poverty, the thrill of waking up to find an orange on her pillow at Christmas. Or a toddler (her first-born) she'd sent out to play while she finished vacuuming, and the helpless horror a few minutes later, finding that child drowned.

For eight years she commuted 120 roundtrip miles to class from the cabin she and her husband and two kids built board by board up near the Canadian border, where they lived with no electricity, few other comforts, and a giant trampoline just outside the front door because whatever space Brenda occupied, she made some fun of it. She was the kind of student that makes a job like mine worthwhile; she was talented, prolific, bright-eyed in class and eager to learn, squeezing out poems between keeping her family afloat in the wilderness, organizing a girl scout troop, and teaching gymnastics. And she became a terrific poet, to the point where I was learning from her at least as much as I could offer in return. In time she'd compiled ample credits to earn an Associate of Arts degree and jangled and twirled across the stage at graduation. Then came a bachelor's degree through a distance learning program, and when she finished that—the last I saw of her—she triumphantly jumped up and down in my office doorway with news she'd been admitted to the graduate writing program at the University of Montana. Dear Reader, brace yourself: Brenda Nesbitt died in a head-on crash commuting to Missoula, her first semester of enrollment. Many grieved and are still grieving. Brenda's poem "Mother's Day 1996" was written shortly before her death that same year. In her box below my desk is a damaged disk of irretrievable poems . . . labeled "Book One."

A gentle giant, when Irvin Moen sat in our circle of writers, he slumped a little forward in his chair and hunched his shoulders, careful he didn't take up too much space, and still he filled the room. On and off for more than a decade, he brought his poems to class and sat humbly waiting his turn, quiet for the most part, but when he spoke we all listened closely. Irvin had a knack for breathing life into his classmates' poems. His voice wavered when he talked, his large hands trembled, and his face flushed a rosier glow than usual, as if something in him waited to explode and he choked it back. Always his words were soft, full of compassion for any human frailty. He wrote tight-fisted narratives about his struggles with mental illness, an affliction that crippled him till his last breath. He wrote love poems to his wife, and poems about homelessness and addiction. Poetry was his life raft in the dangerous seas of therapy, medication, and incarceration. For months he'd disappear from us, and then I'd get a phone message, always polite, telling me he'd written new poems, wondering if he were still welcome to join us, as if he needed our forgiveness for his absence. When his mind was balanced, he craved adventure, skydiving and rock-climbing, and we all felt glad for him . . . and knew it wouldn't last. He phoned me from Warm Springs State Hospital; I ached to make sense of his slurred speech. "It's the drugs," he'd say, "the goddamned drugs." Sometimes I avoided his calls, and that must have hurt, but he never let on. He'd phone again. He published several dozen poems in respected journals. He died in his early fifties. His wife, Wren, carefully gathered his poems and cataloged them alphabetically in binders. There's at least a couple books' worth, and had he lived longer, these books might have found a publisher, won awards.

Aunda Cole was no ordinary little old lady. She reminded me of a butterfly, so delicate her movements, so faint her comings and goings; her small feet seemed to barely touch the earth. She, too, brought her pages to our classroom for many years, poems about her long-deceased barnstorming pilot husband, about dance and music, about the wonders of the Montana wilderness. When she read her poems about her husband and his fly-boy cronies, her face lit with a mischievous spark. She'd loved a daredevil flyer, and there was an inextinguishable streak of wildness in her, too, into her seventies and eighties. An avid back-country hiker, she could recount the details of every turn on dozens of trails in Glacier National Park, including encounters with wildcats and grizzlies. She knew the names of flowers, trees, birds, and rocks, and honored these names in her poems as if she were speaking of friends and neighbors. If

I crabbed at a young student in class, or criticized someone's poem too harshly, she'd wrinkle her brow, look over at me, and shake her head disapprovingly. When she died, her daughter, Diana, had asked me to read Shelley and Keats (Aunda's favorites) at the gathering after the funeral service, but I'd misunderstood and came unprepared. Aunda's poems were displayed at a nearby table, so I reached and read some of Aunda's verses. I shivered to hear the very same poems I'd passed over without careful enough notice in class, now in my voice, on my tongue. "Open your eyes," the poems insisted, reminding us to rejoice, to sit with her on a rocky ledge and just be still. Be here. Be now. Sad that it took me till then to open my eyes to the profundity of her unassuming songs.

So this anthology is dedicated to these three memorable poets who in this isolated place made a community in the classroom. Theodore Roethke wrote, "I tend to grade those students most highly who take their job of educating me most seriously." Brenda, Irvin, and Aunda never gave a frog's fart about their grade. They came to class those years because they were filled with a passion for poems, which is something not many people share, so we were glad to find each other. And, yes, they educated me, their teacher.

How many other Brendas and Irvins and Aundas out there in the sagebrush write and go on writing despite rural isolation and few of the opportunities for advancement and recognition available elsewhere? This anthology soon outgrew our original intention to include 100 poets. About a dozen well-known writers graciously offered poems: Jim Harrison, John Haines, Patricia Goedicke, James Welch, Robert Pack, Madeline DeFrees, Richard Hugo, and others. We welcomed their support. In the sixteen months it took to move this anthology from idea into reality, news of this project spread across the state, and our list of poets and poems grew. Alas, though we've tried our mightiest to be inclusive, surely we have missed someone. If that's you, please forgive us.

Walt Whitman savored the "blab of the pave." He had an ear for the beauty—and necessity—of a multiplicity of voices. Dana Gioia, in his now-famous essay "Can Poetry Matter?" articulated strategies to build audiences for poetry. He advised poets not to hog the stage with only their own voices, their own poems, but instead to share the spotlight by reading also the works of others, including worthy voices which hadn't yet found much exposure. It's in this same spirit that this anthology opens space to the words of many lesser-known names among names already acclaimed. I am especially proud to present so many Native American poets in these pages, including poems in several Native languages. I am hopeful, too, that this collage of voices will help dispel some of the myths and stereotypes about Montanans. We do have bathrooms and electricity. Well, most of us. May these poems, in their mixed perspectives, circle near the truth of our daily lives. It is an honor, reader, to bring you these many voices.

We are Many Voices Press.

Lowell Jaeger
Bigfork, Montana
May, 2007

Photo by Philip Maechling

Sandra Alcosser

The Meadowlark, The Mother

Who spreads feathers over a nest in flames—
The meadowlark, the mother, first container

Of the alphabet, the village, the inch.
Our face water on which her face exists.

Something grew into her that would not leave
The mineral of the race, its meter.

And so when a mother falls, we become her.
How mothers fall as families before her.

Bones grow airy as gothic cathedrals.
Leave me, she says, her eyes derange the wall.

What will we do with you darling when we
Must let you go? Our atoms mostly empty

Space—when will another come along to
Cradle us—in the way that humans do?

Cry

White legs and pink footpads, the black cat
loved me. It was summer, a perfect flush
of weeds and flowers. Mornings he'd listen
for my kettle, the screen door snap, and he'd know
I'd come to breakfast in the asters. As I ate
a bowl of red berries, he'd burl and stretch
and claw about my hips.

One night as the cat and I watched the moon eclipse
amid the scuttling of bear and mice, there was a cry
from the forest, not seductive, but pained and wailing
like a siren. The next day the cat was gone. I'd heard
that even blackbirds broke veins in their throats
singing love songs. I stood by my window practicing,
trying to shape the feline song, to call him back.

My daughter was no different than a cat,
tapping the window glass over my bed,
crying at night till I rocked her frail ribs
against mine. Her hands on my breast,
dark curls sweated against her forehead,
tell me about the princess, she said, the way
she slept in a blue dress, waiting.

It was a month of heatstorms, lightning scratched
like Sanskrit across the valley. A boy came riding
our footpath. He wore black jeans, a sliver of green
malachite at his neck. The breathless afternoon,
the bees laid out on the red eyes of gaillardia.
Before she left my daughter cut off her long hair
and bleached it yellow.

There were years when I too turned from my mother's
cool white arms. First the pale boy, scarred
and silent, then my husband. We cleaned the ditches
together in spring, raking out the silt and dead branches.
He played a silver harmonica. A ring-boned pony
was what I had when we ran away. A field of salsify
and a black skillet.

Stretched out on the porch this noon, resting
my swollen legs, I'm tired of canning tomatoes,
the house thick with red steam and basil.
The bite of salt and vinegar, cucumbers
floating like green bathers in brine.
All that flesh I've tended gone to pulp.
All that mismatched tenderness.

One weed knows another and each animal has its own cry
and when it's right, it's easy. Easy as my husband
behind me now, holding open the black screen door.
He is drinking tea with honey and a halo of gnats
screams about his face. Let's sneak down to the basement,
he says, where it's cool and dark. He cracks a bead of ice
in his teeth and offers half to me.

A Valentine

Near midnight the long awaited snow
fell for awhile and then departed,
leaving behind a little dust of kisses,
coldest lightest kisses on the broken-hearted
sidewalk. Wind came, blew them away–
away, too, the wind. Calm, then cloud, moon gartered
with a hazy ring of frost, the whole sky
overcast and lit from beneath by bartered
light from the windows of buildings: a slow
janitor finishing his rounds, the last plant watered,
the last floor polished. Late traffic sighs
along the streets, some radio crackles hatred
into our weary ears: car bombs, gray
forecasts of famines, another flood, poison-darted
words. I think of snow, its near misses,
its fly-bys, how it keeps standing us up like a hard-hearted
lover, its scent like perfume lingering in the air: how love
is the arm I would slip over your shoulder,
gently, as we walk the alleys in the snow
that isn't falling – all those broken promises
of air and light and earth, all of us older
than we ever could have imagined, our careful charted
way a tangle of missteps. No matter:
Here's to any weather that the cat drags in.
Here's to love, again.

Epłčť eť ʔu Sčilip

Dixon wasn't always known for its only bar.
It was a place the Pend d' Oreille
would go for plums. In its name
its purpose, *plums at junction of two rivers.*

Where the Jocko pours itself
into the Flathead, the trees,
heavy with deep purple fruit,
grew in excess. Their limbs
hung low to the ground,
under the weight of their world.

Over-ripe plums like so many things
dropped to a life of decay. The second
they fell they began to die. The end
of one life, the beginning of another.
It was a place
where plums were known to grow.

Pendant Watch

In Missoula, Montana, where the townsfolk water
the sidewalks, and the Clark Fork River barely interrupts
the usual flow of traffic on Higgins Avenue, I pass,
outside a furniture store, the world's largest
captain's chair. In it sits the world's largest captain,
native to Montana, foursquare and friendly,
with a timeless eye trained on the University
while the mountain flashes holding heaven
in a mist the rest of us steer clear of.

Still agile at forty-odd, I could shinny up
that walnut leg to lie in the lap of the god,
call him husband or lover, warm as any woman in a clockwork
swoon. Except that some more concentrated fire balanced
the cogs, married gut to metal. Today's AP wire
ticks off: Nun Burns Self to Death, and in eight-point type
from Saigon, a Buddhist virgin goes out in sheer fire
while I splutter cold a spark at a time.

Time hangs golden at my breast, a decoration in disrepair
that may not run much longer. Still, I am there beside
that well-regulated throne or bed, not altogether dead.
And the captain knows. And I know. We have it timed to the
                                                    second.

The Past Has No Dwelling Place

It's simple. When you left, I began to hide
inside my body, and when I began to hide
my body, you left. This afternoon the light
strikes the garbage can and the mare,
torn from her colts, rears and paws.

I yank the reins and circle tighter, her
muzzle frothing at my knee, left eye
gone white. Her body in my hand again,
we blow through whatever's in the way,
air, heat, clouds like giant brains—

violent intimates ripping a hole in the woods,
the scent of leaf mold, moss, last year's
spongy mire escapes. At the ditch
she springs from foot to foot, so elegant,
so sly I want to be her shadow draped

over downed trees, gliding through
ravines where trilliums and calypsos rise,
colors smeared by dusk and speed, headlights
caught in the trees. As if God were ahead,
we skid to a stop just at the blacktop's edge.

A voice says: "I'd rather die like this,"
my nose against her aromatic neck.
Together we are separate, delicate,
and bold. Suddenly she's desperate
for her colts, whinnying in the dark.

It's all approach and no arrival. You won't
be kneeling in the garden as I sponge
the bridle. You were a man without particular
love for horses, pulling up the corn,
tossing it into the crib for the colts to eat.

Montana Pears

In the middle of Montana, eating.
What the man sliced for them, two pears on a plate
sprinkled with bottled lime juice
and sugar.

His fork. Then hers. Spearing up
naked, white-to-sour-green
chunks of moonless November's
cold orchards.

Tired, both of them.
On the thick, green
chemically textured part nylon
and wool sofa.

The man's comfortable
beige sweater bulges
next to the woman stuffed
into cheap stretch pants, a faded
apple red Tee shirt.

Eighty years old.
And sixty. Add or
subtract a few. What have they been doing
all those years?

You, out there in the dark,
don't be afraid.
See, they're all lit up for you, do you
know them? I don't,
and I'm stage manager here. In fact,
I'm one of the actors.

A tape purrs in the background.
As the man forks up
the last piece of pear and puts it
in the woman's mouth,

Mark Daterman's electric guitar wheedles
over Glen Moore's acoustic bass in
The Blimp Wars, two state-of-the-art
instruments plucking, twining around each other.

The next piece they play is named after William
Carlos Williams' *The Great Figure*, in gold
reedy overtones, crackling halos of twanged
glowing noise, but then Daterman

and Moore stop playing, the man
says something, the woman nods,
thanks the man for the pears, I think he
thanks her for the music.

Pleased, both of them
peer at their books again.
But even the smartest, new
chemical preservatives can't help:

crushed, folded in on themselves
like sausages,
all the orchards are dark now, cold
shadowy fruit lumped
in heaps on the bare ground.

Silence. Then she stretches,
tucks her stockinged feet
in his lap. He strokes them
without looking, pauses
every once in a while to stare, rub his eyes
with the back of his hand. Well,

it's ten o'clock.
Soon they'll be going to bed.
Does the telephone ring? Doesn't anyone
recognize them? You, out there in the dark,
look in at the two of them,
glowing.

Gretel Alone

Call these woods a cage and you wouldn't
be so far wrong—sun long gone
by late afternoon and town farther.

Trees fall for no reason, just their own weight
pulling them moaning down. I keep a list
of untraceable sound—a giggle of water,

a drum, something, or someone, bawling.
Beyond the meadow, nothing but thornbrush
and a bad smell. Who taught me these rules—

don't walk in the white fog that fills
the valley and rises like a smothering
dough. Don't touch the white foam

that bubbles from certain plants like the mouth
of a rabid dog. Whose whisper says build
a necklace from the bleached spine of a bird,

the hollow globe of a wasp gall, smooth
and weightless, but stringed inside? A woman
in an alley puts her hand through the dark

of a barred window and stands still a long
time. A child holds the woman's free hand,
red candy plugging her mouth, the tall window

empty as a blind eye. I walk the trail
to the river with a metal rake, peeling back
layers of moss and leaves. I snag vines

and tear them free, roll rocks to the edge
and push them over. Do I mean to preserve
the trail or obscure it, as I step backward

in a cloud of stinging gnats, erasing
my footprints as I go? In a breeze a rain
of needles falls. I am half a story.

Vireo

And although I am afraid for the soil and silver hills,
for the root systems and breath systems, for those

who feed under cover of night, there is still a strange
borderless joy in the upper rooms of trees, as vireos

sail between branches, bobbing through the swept
white sky, acquainted with cloud-drift and the evermore

intricate breezework of space. A reverie
of hollow bones and strong taut feathers that whisk and

pivot with our eyes' vitality, they elude each specific death
as hawks move like light through smoke, hanging without sound.

Innocents, the day has brought you everything you need,
and the depths that open up beneath you are of no

concern to you—the phlox growing up the rotting shed,
the slow scuttle of cars, each hometown blinking through

exhaust as the evening broods then descends.
We fail where you most survive, at the brink of air, pushing

hard against the pressures of the given. What do you
have, coming suddenly where all things are?

Reading Novalis in Montana

The dirt road is frozen. I hear the geese first in my lungs.
        Faint hieroglyphic against the gray sky.

Then, the brutal intervention of sound.
        All that we experience is a message, he writes.

I would like to know what it means
        if first one bird swims the channel

across the classic V, the line flutters, and the formation dissolves.
        In the end, the modernists must have meant,

it is the *human* world we are weary of,
        our arms heavy with love, its ancient failings.

But this is before the world wars, in 1800,
        when a young German poet could pick at the truth

and collect the fragments in an encyclopedia of knowledge.
        There is a V, then an L, each letter

forming so slowly that the next appears before it is complete.
        The true philosophical act is the slaying of one's self,

Novalis writes and dies, like Keats, before he is thirty.
        They have left me behind like one of their lost,

scratching at the gravel in the fields. Where are they
        once the sky has enveloped them?

I stand in the narrow cut of a frozen road leading into mountains,
        the morning newspaper gripped under my arm.

But to give up on things precludes everything.
        I am not-I, Novalis wrote. *I am you.*

If, as the gnostics say, the world was a mistake
        created by an evil demiurge, and I am trapped

in my body, abandoned by a god whom I long for as one of my own,
        why not follow the tundra geese into their storm?

Why stay while my great sails flap the ice
        as if my voice were needed to call them back

in the spring, as if I were the lost dwelling place for the flocks?

Rattlesnake, Icicle

I had a long question when I headed to the river.
It was a question of desire, and losing everything in one year.
I passed a skin, unsheathed with no rattle.
I passed a broken icicle fallen from a barn.
The river was as electric as a man's back, risen from the bed.
The river was a scurrying rat.
Across the river a fisherman dropped his cast, hard wrist, line like a halo
over his head. The man was an archangel, or at least espoused the archangel's
philosophy of catch and release.
When I left for my walk, I was bereft. But this is winter in Montana:
you find the dead, you find abandoned skins, you find a doe
frozen, wide-eyed, a delicate rime over its fur. You find a man in the high sun,
with no hope of catching anything, caught off season, but on the river for the solitude
of the snake long gone, for the sharp icicle's drop, for the doe, hard, soulless
in the grass. I had a long question when I headed to the river.
It was about paradise. It was about finding everything again.

Mountain Meditation

The snow-topped mountain range
across the eastern sky,
electric blue as dusk comes on—
that is the view I've chosen
now that old age shapes my needs,
the view my study window
in the house we had our son design
looks out upon as if it were
an inner view into myself as well.
Late winter afternoons
sunlight upon the heaped-up snow
transforms the blazing white to blazing pink,
then darkens into purple
with its own internal glow.
Indifferent, austere, spectacular,
devoid of meaning to console
upon which I can meditate, I dwell
upon the human history of cruelty,
so vast that it defies depiction, yet
I still believe somehow
ultimate destruction might be
avoidable, controlled
by kindness, what at best we are, unlike
tornados, floods, or hurricanes,
earthquakes, and epidemics, accidents.
But surely what I wish cannot be true,
hatred and war, vindictiveness,
must be as much a part of nature
as the seasons are,
and even if a lawful god designed it so,
I cannot worship him;
I won't allow myself to long
for immortality of any kind—
even a universe
where in some obscure place
pulsating life can make itself at home.
I close my eyes and picture suns
collapsing and extinguishing themselves
in space that thins to nothingness;
I see a summer cricket silenced
beneath his once protecting stone.
And yet I am consoled, at least in part,
or partly so, by late vermilion light
now changing on the mountain peaks,
because I choose to make this spectacle
signify what I am,
because for now it's here,
as you and I are here—as if that's all
we need to know, trembling together
in the impersonal, chill air
of the transfigured mountain's afterglow.

Elegy For Jim Welch

Over the tree tops, a big empty blue.

A mourning dove calls, *where are you?*

Twin whitetail fawns lie in the shade
of cottonwoods near the irrigation ditch
we crossed, a little drunk, one dark winter
night years ago, your hands on my shoulders,
Lois' hands on yours—the blind leading the blind,
someone said, all of us laughing.

Now a young fox, light August red, stops
at the edge of shade and holds unmoving
as though posed mid-stride by a taxidermist,
except for the eyes which shift their focus
through dappled light of the hawthorn thicket
with a fierce precision, and except for the black
nostrils that sample and sort the layered scents
of morning air—faint musk of deer droppings,
dusty fluff from a finch's abandoned nest,
the nitrogen aura of decaying duff above
interlaced roots of pine and wild pear,
scent-sparks of shell chips left by the pheasant's
hatchlings, and traces of human presence
still pooling in footprints.

The dove calls, *where are you, you you*

out beyond the blue, stars wait to fall.

The fox, a long pause between breaths,
stands poised on three legs in the sun,

then, like a gust of red wind, turns
through the leaves and is gone.

Grounding

Already mid-summer and you have been gone
too long,   untethered,
spinning in a fever to gather twigs and twine,

spin a warm place to set a winter baby.
You are potting plants, making banana bread.

Somehow these things have become urgent.
But listen, this child is not a house guest

it is not a bent-kneed soldier, waiting for ambush,
nor a light-bound answer to anything.
It has no intention
                        and blooms without consent, so stand

still, let gravity do its work. You can't hear
through its ears. You can't see
the lurching of blood and skin.
It grows without fever,
cannot see its own fingers fanning out,
does not know this   as its beginning.

Come away from that moment,
the stretching skin and hot bellowing

red,   then new and slipping like a plum
from ripe skin.
                        Come back
to sounds in the kitchen below, dry toast
sliding across a plate, water on, off,
            the neighbor's dog,   the trains
            braking in the rail yard.

Come back to the strange brightness
of your own weather.
                        Map it again,
as you have one hundred times before
and claim it, simply.

Find your feet touching the ground.
They are beautiful for touching the ground.

The Other Woman

In some things
the body is ahead
of the mind:
the rhythmic motion
over skis
pure primitive dance
as snow blows and curls
to unfixed forms,
tall skinny ghosts
trickle down the air.

The hill falls away.
I am out of my mind
entirely
on the edge of my life,
tottering, half blind
with the gift of
flight
but upright,
a mad bird
dashing towards
that other woman.

So this is what it is
to ride
a beam of light
and meet oneself
and this to fall
free,
not die but lie
breathless in
a great disaster of
trees and
skinful of snow.

She bends over, laughing,
Says, "Remember me?"

Sonnet

She goes, she is, she wakes the waters
primed in their wave-form, a flux of urge
struck into oneness, the solid surge
seeking completion, and strikes and shatters

and is its fragments, distinction's daughters—
and now, unholding, the cleave and merge
the hew and fusing, plundering the verge
and substance is the scheme it scatters

and what it numbers in substantial sun.
Her hands hold many or her hands hold none.
And diving the salt will kiss a convex eye

and be salt fact and be the bodied sky
and that gray weight is both or beggared one,
a dead dimensional, or blue begun.

Photo by Kent Ord

Roger Dunsmore

Girl Dancing in the Green Grasses

I have seen the flower petals
laid upon the eyes
of my dead friend,
seen them waft up
in the slight breeze from a woman's
skirt. I have seen the rot
emerging from his open eye,
and heard the fly
buzzing upon his sheet.
And I have shoved his body
as far into the brick-lined kiln
as my body could reach,
and placed one cigarette upon it
and closed the door and heard
the gas jets roar 1500 degrees
as they melted him down
to a few pounds of ash.

For months
I have written no poem
but I have heard the clanging
of the green, steel door
as the one-ton bison batters it,
and batters it until blood flows
freely from his nostrils.
Quiet then, I have seen him
quiver in the steel cage,
every muscle and nerve,
and heard the school children exclaim
at the green paint upon his broken horn.

I have seen a young girl
dance on the green grass
where drums rumble like hooves,
and her aunt bring a bright-colored
blanket to place beneath her feet.
And I have seen an old woman, heavy,
waddle out from the crowd
to receive that blanket
filled by the young girl's warmth.

For months, I have written no poem
but I have seen these things:
the slight breeze from a woman's skirt,
the green paint upon the broken horn
and a young girl's feet
dancing a blanket full of flowers
for an old woman's arms.

Dog Spelled Backwards

(for Max, born under the juniper and pinion pine wood pile
at Hopi Third Mesa in a snow storm, Thanksgiving Day,
1988, to Twister, his blue heeler mother)

I miss my old dog
when I hear the garbage truck
clanging in the alley
and there is no one to bark at it,
except me.

I miss my dog
when I see Jenni's pizza crust
left on her plate and no one to eat it,
no one to lick out the bowl
used for making enchiladas,
except me.

I miss my old dog
when it is thirty below zero
and there is no one but me
to go photograph the frozen river.

I will miss him in the summer
when there is no one to lie on
the blanket between my feet
in the bottom of the canoe,
not even me.

I miss him
when I'm swimming across the lake
so much slower than all the others
and no one dog-paddles back
to check on me.

My dog had fleas, **never**
but he loved to roll in dead fish
and smell like a rotten toe.
Not me.

He'd let me brush him out
on spring days for just so long
before he'd threaten and sputter
and nip at my hands,
get up and walk away.

He left his hair all over our house,
on rugs, on our clothes, in the car,
little white balls of hair in
the corners of the bedroom.
Not me.

I miss my old dog
when the house creaks
and I think it is him
up walking around
or moaning.
Not me.

It must be good to miss someone so.
I guess that's why
I put his ashes under the Christmas tree.
I guess that's why
when you turn it around,
G-o-d spells dog.
Not me.

Mountain Ash

(for Henry Bugbee)

Hearing that you have died,
I step out my door.
The neighborhood crows squawk
    in the spruce trees
and a flock of wax-wings descends
like a swarm of bees
onto mountain ash berries
hung in silent brilliance.

There were no words the last time,
only my awkwardness,
your determination.
You touch the smooth skin of your cheek,
the beard you had grown shaved off,
the family coming in for a final visit.
You stare into my eyes.
I hold your gaze.
When I say my name,
ask if you know me,
you extend your hand.
I take it.
You squeeze firmly.
Your gaze is not "hollow,"
as someone put it,
though many small strokes
have done their work.
I touch the smooth skin of your cheek.

Ed said my photo of the crippled man
on his four wheeled cart in Loyang,
his blue enamel bowl dangling from an axle,
looked like you.
You hung the photo in your kitchen.

The end of that summer,
sitting in your arbor,
"Were you run through the mill
while you were in China?" you ask.

Yes. And you know what did it?
Massage.
A fourth generation Chinese masseur

bore down so hard
with these three fingers
I thought he had an iron tripod in his hand.
The next day I nearly passed out after class.
My Chinese colleagues laughed.
Later I got the flu,
and after two weeks, pneumonia,
twenty-four days in a Chinese hospital,
on intravenous.
I was afraid I was going to die.
That massage released fifty years
of stored up trash in my being.
I wasn't ready for that.

Maybe you were...ready.

Well...I didn't die.

Here, here....

You raise your first glass of ale
for the day, old teacher and friend
I have not come often enough to see.
We drink to this not dying,
your eyes like a cat's
there in the sheltered arbor
those last days of summer.

Now there are no words.
These crows, this wind-chime,
open a door.
A soft breeze blows
your wax-wing heart
into the brilliant silence
of mountain ash.

Naming The Unknown

I know
                none of their names

but they are

>   the Down-River-Riders-To-The-Sea
>   the Up-On-The-Next-Wave Steppers
>   the Tumbled-In-Surf-Black Feathers
>   or Orange-Long-Beaks-Snoozing-On-The-Rocks.
>   They are the Air-Drifting-Skimmers
>   The Diving-In-the-Foam-Floaters
>   the Long-Legged-Feeders-In-The-Froth.

I do not know
                their names
but they are

>   the Three-Toed-Print-Makers-In-the-Sand
>   the Around-the-Warf-Eaters-Of-Garbage
>   the White-Shitters-On-Roof-Tops.

They are

>   the Spray-Flung-Off-Furthest-Breakers
>   the Strung-Across-Blue-Sky-Cloud-Wisps
>   the Breath-I-Cannot-See.

They are the Moon-Sailing-Beneath-A-Single-Star,
the Squawk-Inside-The-Seed.

Navajo Springs

(For James Peshlakai)

Three birds leave a tamarisk tree,
three birds as if they are one,
and the flick of a lizard
into a cracked boulder,
quickest motion,
like the stone's mouth,
like its tongue.
This lizard licks
uranium mine tailings
leaching into the water
above Moenkopi Village.

When the government standards
are read at the public hearing:
Place an earth and cement cap
over the tailings that will last
for a thousand years,
the company men smile slightly:
A thousand years?
We won't be here, this company.
Why, even this government…

A small man from the village
raises his hand:
A thousand years, he says.
We'll be here.

We buy corn from a man
selling Navajo Bibles too,
Bibles mixed in with corn the color of sky
tumbled in the back of his truck.
Home, he says,
is a clean heart,
turquoise washed by rain
for a thousand years.

Aurora Borealis

(for Jenni)

We walk the dog together
for the first time in weeks.
Eerie streaks of light
waver the sky.
We spin round and around,
our heads bent back,
watching green radiance
dissolve and reappear
like signs in some forgotten tongue.

The dawn is the ancient goddess Aurora.
For her sake, they say,
her husband got the gift of immortality,
but not the gift of youth.
He grew older and older
and uglier and smaller
until he ended up
as a grasshopper.
His green sky.

I remember the day we flipped our boat
on the big lake, the wind blowing it
far down the bay.
You, a fast swimmer, could have
caught up to it.
"Don't leave me!" I cried out,
and we stayed together,
awkwardly working our way
two hours to shore
through cold, choppy water.

We spin now in this mid-night,
northern-dawn gone
all to starry, green streaks,
crazed and comforted--
grinning like two old grasshoppers
in the solar wind.

A True War Story

My friend's uncle
was a Marine in Korea.
His squad came to a cluster of huts,
smoke drifting up from one.
The squad leader ordered him
to go into that hut,
to kill everyone inside.
He stepped cautiously through the doorway
and waited for his eyes to adjust.
In the dim light he saw a terrified Korean woman,
children huddled up against her.
He squeezed the trigger on his M1,
emptied it into the thatched roof,
and stepped back out
through that doorway.
No one spoke.

Back home,
when he told the old people
what he had done,
they gave him a new name:
He-Who-Takes-Pity-On-His-Enemy,
and made him
the giver of names
for new-born children.

drive on

we can't always get engaged in material which i suppose is
part of why life seems so often to suck we suddenly find
ourselves in our fifties crazy about a nineteen year old crazier
than you can remember and discover it's the wrong goddamned
universe like the time isn't there isn't standing still like it should
be like driving to butte late morning on saturday only to discover
the paint store doesn't have the color you need and can't mix
because machine is broken then the cafe that cooks the best
damn roast beef sandwich is closed early and so you give up
and drive through macdonalds hoping not to die and drive
back to dillon then half way need to piss so bad you think about
dangling your ass out the window while driving cruise control
but stop and just as you are ready to let loose the river of life
jesus appears in a vision of a rainbow and it starts snowing
and you just know it's one of those moments not to be ignored
and so you suck it up hold it in and wait to hear the words
gushing out of his goddamn mouth which when they finally do
make no goddamn sense and by the time you realize the
significance had to do with relieving and let go he's gone and
so is the rainbow replaced by red flashing lights a cop his
silver handcuffs dangling at his side baton pointing at your
midsection telling you you'd better get on the way before he
takes you in for indecent exposure if you know what's good for
you and for once you read a situation correctly and instead of
discussing the beautiful essence of the human body even
yours you mutter jesus and hop back into your car and take
off making sure not to speed at least until he's out of mirror
range it never ending so by the time you get home you've held
so long and the damn holy golden liquid won't release and
your belly swells to the size of that pumpkin the kid down the
block carved last halloween in the likeness of hitler and you
wish to hell you'd let loose on the cops polished boots but
didn't that's part of some other narrative it's crazy time can't
shake feelings deep I mean hard all the way to magma
beneath the pacific floor near bangkok ocean depth
description it's impossible but there are rainbows in my attic
at least if not your clit finally letting go saying ah

revolution

(for cathy and rio)

does god have a mother he asks
squinting as he looks up
in the bright sunlight
of our morning walk…
—yes i say
offering no explanation…
—whats her name he asks
—ishtar i say raising my arms
to the heavens…
—what he asks
—nothing i say
pondering only a few of her names
queen of heaven
morning star
perpetual help
mother of mercy
our light & hope…our being…
kneeling down i face him squarely & say…
—where i come from we call her
mother of god
—but who is more powerful he asks
god or his mom…
—well…i say
if you want something done right
youve got to go to the source
—oh he sez then asks…what does she do

—do you mean besides wiping the butt of baby jeezuz…
i ponder this to myself then say
—she loves us & takes care of us
—does she save us from the bad guys
—yes i say…she is the biggest crimefighter
of all.

now i knoe it cant be long…
cuz first he wuz spiderman
& then he wuz robin
& then he wuz batman
& then he wuz superman
& now he sez he is god
but i knoe…it wont be long
before i see him running
arms outstretched
cape flying wildly behind
as he flys akross the universe
of his own front yard
hollering @ the top of his lungs
—i am the mother of god
& all you bad guys
are in trouble…

Item:

(Jay Scott is on death row in Ohio. He is the sixth of eleven children raised in poverty and abuse. Early in life, the children were convicted of juvenile offences—Jay, at age nine, for truancy. Ultimately, one brother was shot dead, another rendered quadriplegic from gunshot wounds. His eldest sister died in a house fire, another sister was killed in an argument, and a third sister killed a brother-in-law in self defense. Jay suffers from mental illness.)

Our family of eleven children
foraged for food
in alleyways
behind grocery stores.

Small dreams pulverized
by rage,
grinding brutality.
Even mine.

Every day I hoped
school would be safe;
every day disappointed.

Voices in the night
haunt
my prison cell.
Cries of sisters
and brothers who
died at the hands of family
and lovers. Why do they reach out
for me?

Everything is fog.
I can't find my way.
Mind disintegrates,
plagued with hallucinations
and depression.

Condemned
to be injected
with poison.

The Harvest/The Healing

Picking Peas…

Hot August day. Motorbike
roars down driveway. Our
daughter clings to your back.
You hold inside a silent roar.
Alone, I pick peas.
Pods surprisingly cool.
Smooth skins pulled taut
over lumps of peas remind
me of my breasts, now with more
than fibrocystic breast disease.
My tears spill.
I keep picking peas. It is time
for their harvest.

The Healer…

Wounded, I lie on my side.
Dozens of metal stitches
pull my chest tight.
Gently, you cuddle your
front to my back. Skin
touches skin. Your fingers
trace my face, my scalp,
my neck, my body. They
touch and probe. You tell me
I am beautiful.
And then you love me.

Wives' Tale

You popped out
like a champagne cork,
my midwife catching you
by one arm
as you hit the floor.

Wise slate eyes,
wide open in accusation,
recognition. Love,
instant and profound.

And the shock of you:
your unfinished, unfused face.
Gashed like a dropped melon,
a skewed Picasso,
a seashell whorl
where Cupid's bow
should be.

An embryonic disturbance, they tell me,
between the fourth and eighth weeks.
What or more I'll never know.

Perhaps the old wives' tales
offer a better account:
I must have eaten a hare,
or looked at one the wrong way,
or ventured out
during a lunar eclipse
without placing a pin
over my belly
for protection.

My son, marked by
a hare offended,
the dangerous moon.

Seduction of the Undercurrent

"Friend, do not come in here without desire."
– Paul Valéry

Touch the underbellies of the shear water birds.

Carve his name in the shipboard.

You are no longer the shore worn mouth. Follow the rising loons to the island—our longing is barefoot, hardly speaking.

I mouthed the poem pulsing on his neck. There is another poem rising in the fisherman's quickening breath. We were writing lines as if they belonged to us.

And he read from the blue laws. And he resisted. His tongue kept reaching for my tongue.

Before the mast is the language of not asking and not telling: a desire, not your desire, a body, not a ship-rigged body.

I have washed through his obsessions: the down feathers, the echoes of lapping and whale song, the figurehead carved in the bow of his reaching mouth.

I could hum the song of him by watching the swallowing tide. He blinked rapidly as if motion brought our bodies nearer.

I have washed through the pulsing.

The language of desire: tongues loose in the ink of the other. We spoke at the same time as if we were touching.

Call it carving. Call it entanglement. Call it galaxies of sand. I have explored the ship beds and have too been harmed.

We are the imperfection in the light. We are harlot and the kitchen table.

I turned his hand over and over searching for the words to enter.

He spoke the waters of Zion, and we (*the chosen ones*) turned inward.

I tasted the smoke on his tongue. These things are not connected, and yet they remain on my lips.

Call it want. Call it within. Call it wholeness. Parting. The oyster. The opening. The sound of your own body becoming. It is the language we never speak.

A lover is a sheet anchor. My arms the rising and falling of the lines. I am not beautiful in this way. His touch was a path to remembering.

The water has not want to drown.

The lover, *he* hums the pulse of the pressing wings.

He has come to rest in the open palm.

Germany

(for Senna)

We picked lilacs in tumbling familiar fragrance
and the river rose over its banks,
flowed against the stone steps.
It was your mother's birthday
and we walked together down to the night river.

Three years seemed like so many,
but even if her flame green eyes were closed,
even if they took her body away before you could see it,
you were still in the quiet momentum of her living
like wind blowing a flock of sparrows over the marsh.

You were still moving the pattern of her body,
the pattern of your imperfect mother,
the shape you cut into her
like two leaves packed tight together in the seed.

She had been gone long enough,
but now bound together in sleep
under her down comforter,
we dream the same image of her red hair
so close it wakes us both
in thin dark air, unfamiliar all around us.
You still remembered the smell of her
not with your mind, with your nose,
this mother I never knew, but through your being motherless.

She is as perfect and missing to me
as the unraveling she left in you.

We sat on the steps by the river, in that strange country
eating ice-cream and holding rolled cigarettes
in our young hands.
Yellow boat lights shivered up the current,
into the forked goose tracks in black mud,
the bright tears, thin yellow tares in your eyes.

Tonight something in those city lights
swims up this dark Montana river.
The smell of rain on stones,
broken yellow light
and years we've swallowed up like water.

The Time of Irises

There is the dark one
with that sheen
of fluorescent green
the impossible color
of a male mallard's neck in sun.
And there is the salmon one
I want to call it champagne,
but it is deeper
and more liquid
as though the petals
have drunk the salmon's blood.
And these colors bleed through
just under the surface
of my father's thin Swedish skin
the bruise acquired by pedaling
too far on a stationery bike.
There is also the long green
tube of stem
that so erectly holds up
those ridiculous flowers
five at a time
confident until a heavy rain
crushes down the wet ruffled weight.
And there is the green tube
food-colored in case of choking
that goes into my father's belly
maintaining his fragile weight.
There is no time
to paint the iris this year.
I have become the heavy paper
soaking up the colors
making a wash of the passing Spring.

The Eye In The Rock

A high rock face above Flathead Lake,
turned east where the light
breaks at morning over the mountain.

An eye was painted here by men
before we came, part of an Indian face,
part of an earth
scratched and stained by our hands.

It is only rock, blue or green,
cloudy with lichen,
changing in the waterlight.

Yet blood moves in this rock,
seeping from the fissures;
the eye turned inward, gazing back
into the shadowy grain,
as if the rock gave life.

And out of the fired mineral
come these burned survivors,
sticks of the wasting dream:

thin red elk and rusty deer,
a few humped bison,
ciphers and circles without name.

Not ice that fractures rock,
nor sunlight, nor the wind
gritty with sand has erased them.
They feed in their tall meadow,
cropping the lichen a thousand years.

Over the lake water comes this light
that has not changed,
the air we have always known...

They who believed that stone,
water and wind might be quickened
with a spirit like their own,
painted this eye that the rock might see.

NAMÂTA'SOOMÂHAVEME HE'TOHE HE'KONÔTSE
WE ARE THE SPIRITS OF THESE BONES

Nataosee'eše hae'eševe'ohtsemo'tanonêstse
We have been with these bones for a long time

naa ovahe nataašeasehetotaetanome hestsêstseahe
and we are beginning to feel a whole lot better now

he'tohe he'konôtse tse'eševa ho'êho'êtseto hetseohe tsetsêstâhase
tsêstaomepo'anomevôtsevôse he'tohe ho'e.
that these bones are back among the Cheyenne people on their Reservation.

Naa ova matohe nahotoanavetanome.
But we are troubled for another reason.

Na'omeaseohtsetanome
We want to travel on

He'tohe he'konôtse etaešeeva ovana'xaahe no'oma'enenêstse.
now that these bones are safely buried.

Oxesta etaaševa hešeovêšemanenêstse.
They have now been properly put to rest.

Henehe nêhetao'e etaaše nêšepêheva'e.
All that has happened is all very good.

Hetohe he'konôtse etaešenêšekanome evapêhevo'tanêstse
These bones are now in a good place.

Naaova naso'e hotovanavetanome:
But we are still troubled:

Naa taamahe tsemâhta'soomâhavetse hetseohe
Tsexho'eohtsanetse nasaahestâheme.
We as the spirits do not know this place.

Hetseohe na'ohkeva'neamesohpeohtseme heva
We just used to travel through this place when

ho'e ve'otsêtse naa matôhova ho'e eemôhonetse.
we were hunting the enemy or hunting for food.

Hetseohe nasaahestâhaheme, nešêhene'enome.
We are not from here, we want you to know that.

Hetsêsteahe naoveamemano'eeme.
We have been meeting and singing.

Emâhemoheevameo'e tse'tohe mâhta'soomaohe.
All the spirits who have been with these bones for a long time were called to a meeting to sing songs.

Nanôhtsenanonôtse ho'nehenoonôhotse tsetao'seevâne'evaotsêhaatse Ma'ta'omeaseohtsêtse.
We are looking for the right wolf songs that will guide us.

Hetsêstseahe naohkenemeneme.
So now we are singing.

Naohkeonesehahtsenonêstse nemeohtôse.
We are trying different songs.

Ma'tahe me'enomatse, nêtseo'omeaseohtseme,
Whenever we find the right wolf songs,

hapo'e tosa'e nêtseovêšename, tosa'e tsehpevêhene'enomatse.
we will travel on to a place we know, to a familiar place where we can sleep peacefully.

Tsetaosêsaaevave'êšehavesevetanohostse.
Where we will no longer feel bad.

Tsetaosêsaaevave'êše hoonêsetanohostse.
Where we will not feel so homesick.

"Taxa'e netaoneseme'enanonôstse nemeotôtse," naheme.
"Let us find our wolf songs so we can journey on," we said.

Navemaamahmovananonêstse onehavo'êstse. Henehe navemanêstsenonêstse.
We also put together some hand drums. That's what we were doing.

Henehe komaa'se navepo'ponâhanonêstse.
That's what we were drumming on.

Naa hetsêtseahe naeveno'nêtseanonêstse nemenêstôtse tsetaase
And now we are finding those songs that we're going to sing as we travel on

ve'êseo'omôhoxovestavatse naa matôhova hetseohe nâtanêšeeveova'na'xaanaotseme.
to where we can sleep peacefully.

He'tohe naonêsaanêšekanome pêhevehene'enahenone.
We do not know this Reservation land very well.

Good Girls Don't Hooky-bob

My mother suddenly appears—
a surprising, unexpected vision
striding on snowy sidewalk
by the Catholic Church.

Gray woolen coat sleeves wrap tight
around two brown grocery bags
and peering over the tops, her face
a startle of downward lines.

Mouthline, eyebrows, even crows feet,
all descend southward as her head
does a quick swivel to track me.
Her mouth a frozen oval.

My red wool mittens never slip
on the rear metal bumper.
Hardpack snow peels up in frosty curls
over the edge of my brown/white
saddle shoes. Feet twist left, then right
and a quick left again to keep
a fragile balance. No time
to raise a mitten in defiant wave.
Knees bounce a low crouch. I fear
how much of me
might appear in the driver's
frosted rearview mirror.
White car exhaust streams
close to my left ear. I gasp.
This Chevy's definitely
picking up speed.

Pleated plaid wool skirt flaps and trails
in the snowy street. How fast
the bare trees fly by. My mother's image
a single frame now gone.

But the too blue day
ablaze with light can't hide
my grin and thrown-back head
as the car puts distance between us.

Photo by Robert Ostler

Tami Haaland

Let Deer Come Crashing

Who knows what makes you leave the table,
walk up hill? In dim light you hear their hooves.
Three deer in velvet cross pavement and climb,
a woman and barking dog chase behind
then turn into the darker part of the street.

City on one side, sage and sandstone above,
your eyes encounter deer eyes. You want
the vision, deer crashing the dark world awake.
They want rabbit brush, cover of dusk to graze.
Have you noticed the night bird's repetitive cry?

Kathy Catches a Train

I am stuck on twenty-seventh street behind three cars
in the turn lane. I am late to meet my friend who walks north
while I drive south so we can meet midway at McCormick Café.

Then the trains come, freighters hauling coal and boards. One train
blocks twenty-seventh and the crossing arms come down.
My light is red, and too much traffic has backed up.

Waiting and waiting. But then, here comes Kathy.
She's been stuck behind that train too, and, impatient now,
she strides past the fallen arms and climbs the engine's stairs.

She wears her brown plaid jacket and I can see she plans to step down
the stairs to this side of the tracks, but the train starts to move.
I see her hold the rail. Afraid to risk falling beneath wheels,

she stays, surprised and still. In a minute, she's behind a brick building
heading west. I wonder if she'll let go of the rail and go inside
or if she'll hang on until they find her and pry her loose. I wonder

when the people at work will realize she hasn't come back from lunch,
and when her husband will find out she hasn't stayed late at the office.
Surely the engineer will offer her shelter as they climb the continental divide.

Trains must have food. I bet they stop sometimes, and she could
get off wherever she likes. Of course I'll hear from her. She'll call
and tell me about the island she inhabits or her winter vacation

in Brazil. I'll tell her how she looked that day, boldly impatient
when her road was blocked, the machine taking her from her settled life.

Chicago, 1959

Through the hot summer twilight
Just this edge of light,
I would rest in the bodies
Of my father, grandfather,
Uncles Tony and Joseph,
On one lap or another
Like the small animal I was.
My face a pebble under
A wood-dark stream
As my lungs released
Cricket by cricket
Into the slow exhilaration
Of a falling sky
As a yellow-bulb
Lantern frame dipped in
And out of my eyes
Swaying as a boat sways
Across the unmeshed
Darkness of the sea.
And I was drawn
Tenderly as blood,
Through the rhythms of their flesh
And the unspoken womb
Of the company of men.

Poem for Insomniacs

We do expire, but not before sips
of crème de menthe and cigarettes.
Just hours ago I was sugared, cheap
as penny candy, a hothouse fruit
and busy as wild belladonna.
In bars long after sunset in February
and the city like a dropped bracelet,
I joined in the activities of the awake:
girlfriends in cars, poker machines,
snapshots and rows of chrome bikes—
far from the objects of insomniacs:
volumes of Shakespeare, sheet music,
the somnolent feasts of broken bread,
a sectioned orange. And what of it?
To say a woman is vibrant, alive,
and beautiful will never compare
to the glamour of the insomniacs—
for days we are over-exposed, kin
to night-blooming things, split
open for consumption by stars,
whole fields of bleached skin
and sweet, swelling bone underneath.

Becoming My Unspoken Name

I am the clatter of aspen
raspy as unclipped artichokes
articulate out of my bare-boned breath
breathless I birth words

raspy as unclipped artichokes
my name begs its utterance
breathless I birth words
the mule and the muse marry

my name begs its utterance
alphabet weds to wonder
the mule and the muse marry
their union carries me under

alphabet weds to wonder
articulate out of my bare-boned breath
their union carries me under
I am the clatter of aspen

COMING UP DAFFODILS

(for my son, Ben)

> "Think of your writing as a conversation you are having with the dead."
>
> Dana Gioia

East Rosebud Valley, Beartooth Mountains, Montana

I accept the sizzle of lightning,
gnarl of thunder, smoke of rain,
terror in a small boy (oh my son, my son),
the scour of wind.
I hoist you shoulder high;
we hold tight against the wayward grays
of late afternoon.

Glen Helen, Yellow Springs, Ohio

Softly, the raw world wakes:
mosses swell from split rock,
squirrels scurry cones to earth,
spiders weave nets of light.
Sinking into needles and leaves,
we breathe wet woods.
One dead possum,
flattened virtually to oblivion,
seems to you
a simple matter of fact.

Escalante roadless area, Utah

In sand-rock country
you walk too long through urging water,
taut muscles grown cold and stiff.
Four of us knead your arms, legs, feet.
Heat restores you,
blood makes you dance,
and the narrowing canyon waits.

Beartooth–Cooke City Pass, Montana

Fifteen miles from open flame,
we camp at lake side.
You help anchor our tent.

We rest.
I admire the fire-pink sun;
you peruse a paperback *Meinkampf*.
Do I know you, who and where you are?
Are you unhappy by still water
in this season of ashes?

Billings, Montana

Dad
Your voice demands
Here I am
In this place at this time
Look at me
I try not to listen
I'm your boy, I'm your boy,
I'm your boy

Burnside Bridge, Willamette River, Oregon

Once upon a drafty drawbridge
stood a man too soon grown sad.
Over and out and down he fell
to a hard wet void. None saw him rise.
Beyond the reach of a chill morning
the water flows, calm and dark.
Flotsam rides the eddies circling,
circling toward the tide-warped sea.

Downtown Portland, Oregon

Tell me, chalky bones,
do you still wander with the street-wise,
the floaters, the drifters?
Below many-storied cliffs,
contrived sidewalks favor cold metal bears,
obese stone cats,
brassy women with gold nipples,
and the daffodils of early spring.

Mt. St. Helens, Washington

I imagined standing with you,
equal to equal,

below the cirque
cradling the lava-lifted bubble of rock.
Just here, a stone wind
cooked high slopes into cement,
shredded whole forests
and one man who waited
to give warning.

South of Columbus, Montana

Bighorns, Pryors,
Beartooths, Crazies
stand, blue-gray in late light.
On a roundy hill,
under a shadowing ponderosa
a slight wind stirs the buffalo grass,
tangling yellow
through earth to sky.
Here and now becomes
a tinkling of pipes.
Far downslope,
a low sun fires the cottonwoods,
the afternoon burns
and, just for a little,
you are everywhere.

from: **Winter Tenor**

Whomsoever is in your house
Becomes your house,
And yet, how much can the body
Accommodate
For one must suffer torsion
To break into the light.
For now, it is summer.
From Lords Valley
To Dingmans Ferry I watch
The advancing rain,
Sheet lightning over low hills
As humidity rides the open ground,
These stones, this field
Not lodged with what-has-been
But what-is-being—
The obese donkey nudging a fence
Waiting for news of any brother,
A rock wall entering a pond,
A burning log-deck,
Siamese cat in the mow-path
Crouching before the blades,
The overgrown road that leads
To your house, wild-dogs
That keep me to this path
And not another
For my god is not calmness
But a stand of birch
Catching flame
As I try to decide what is noun
And what's verb
In the lark's fluted throatings,
Breaking the skin
Of each word I write.

from Notes on Beauty

Girls and boys swoop down—
all sugared up on vanity.

I dare not tell them what I know.

The way beauty empties you out, an immense tide
against your makeshift self, pulling you out into a vast sea
until nothing is left
but a spiraling shadow traced on the sandy beach,

the undertow cut in the shape of divine proportion.

What fine creatures we are
cleared of our little selves
plunged into beauty's ocean
where we dip and bobble
split and sink and come up again and again
as if for air.

Montana Avenue

In the stinking heat of a July afternoon
an Indian finds shade underneath the
protruding neon sign of the pawn shop
and he squats
    leaning against the maroon brick
wall of the building, desperately waiting
to ask someone for change
so he can get a drink at the Empire
where they probably threw him out.
He is looking to find the barkeep's favor by
buying another round
    but he is not having any luck.
He stands with difficulty, begins walking
across the street to sit under a tree
before the dull sandstone building
with the imposing façade.
Later, he goes back to squatting
underneath the sign because
some people he knew came and went.

Northeaster in November

I rushed to lock the chicken house and chase
the cows into the barn. The edge of the wind
was sharp and whipped my scarf across my face;
sometime this afternoon, it changed and thinned
and now blew north by east. The new colt ran
in the corral, eyes wild and tossing head.
His tail and mane straight on the wind as he ran.
I shooed the turkey hens into the shed
and fetched armfuls of wood in from the rick
and piled it high behind the kitchen door.
The rising wind screamed at the eaves and thick
log walls; I checked each window bar before
I looked out on the empty windswept yard
and watched the last dull light of daytime wane.
The first sleet pellets striking hard,
went ricocheting off window-pane.

The Fishing Guide

The fishing guide scrambled
up the sandy river bank,
sore-shouldered from rowing,
thinking of cold beer and big fish.

Behind him, his two clients
followed like tired dogs.
"Soft," he thought in disdain,
just before he was slammed to the earth,
his hat spinning off like a child's toy,
the hot, white light searing his head,
his hip, his heart.

Just for a moment, like us all,
he had taken his eyes off
that little grey cloud on the horizon,
strolled along in the yellow sunlight.

It could just as easily be you or me,
our turn to be hit by a bolt from the blue,
our lives going on or not
as the rain pelts down
and we find ourselves lying alone in the dirt,
our mouths still full of lightning.

Monuments

The relics stand
idle,
monuments to dusty days
and hard-scratch times.
Children wade
through cheatgrass and Russian thistles
to ride on rusty running boards.
Behind phantom wheels
they mouth motor noises,
driving imaginary cargoes
to forgotten elevators—
monuments
to small, warm western towns
that somehow died.

Photo by Amy Jaeger

Lowell Jaeger

Nobody Special

The bus downshifts, strains to climb
around another curve. Another curve.
And one more. I bump shoulders,
with the small man beside me,
when the driver veers right, veers left,
till we get the rhythm of it and lean
on our own without being thrown
side to side.
                    Six hours to the top
of the Sierra Madres. Lurching
and thumping like that. My seat mate
sleeps and wakes. Sleeps more.
Who is he? Needs a shave. Tattered
straw cowboy hat on his lap. Burlap
sack of something heavy on the floor
between his knees. Brown shoes
shaped liked they've known these feet
for as long as he's owned this only pair.

Nobody special. Like the rest
of us; all of us startled awake
when the brakes moan to an unexpected
stop. Engine rattles and coughs.
Who'd believe anyone lives here? Mud
pueblo with no name. Doors fold
open. Hiss closed, and we're off.

Except my seat mate, who waits in the exhaust,
then crosses toward half a dozen niños
who run to greet him, touch palms
to his prickly whiskers and laugh,
the smallest leaping into his arms
so the burlap sack drops . . . and out tumble
oranges enough each child grabs two, three,
while the wind steals
his torn white cowboy hat
which the biggest brother retrieves
for his own head.
                    I look up
for the first time then to the lush
green hills and rocky outcrops
of the tallest peaks beyond,
beyond, beyond. I was wrong
in accounting to you this man. The nobody
special part. You should have seen
the chatter and dust howling
as they all walked toward home.

We All Know Trouble When We See It

Her waitress smock snugs telltale
tight around the middle. Even
the extra apron only makes the problem
more plain. She's "expecting"
and like the lady in the last booth
along the highway window says,
She don't look too happy about it
neither. That's Birdie Jackson
whose son's locked up in Deer Lodge
for shooting his ex-girl and ex-girl's
new guy. Nobody killed nobody.

Plenty of yak, yak, yak
in a town where some people know
everybody's business a whole lot
better than most of us know our own.
Birdie says it in a hissed whisper
to her blue-haired coffee pal. A private
tone, but funny
how the whole place falls quiet
at exactly the right wrong moment
and what's not to be said aloud
gets headlined like big city news.

Birdie's crony nods and sips.
Wanda Whose-Last-Name-I-Forgot.
Tretski. Trotski. Petruski. Like that.
Still owns the Lazy Double H,
at least all what's fenced, but rents
it out now since she's moved to town
after her husband smothered
under a load of manure. Rolled
his John Deere. Bigger story there, too,
the particulars of which could be had
at any table across the room. Asked for or not.

What a shame, Wanda adds,
She's so young. The question
who's the new daddy
drifts in cigarette smoke. Sizzles
on the grill. I catch myself blushing,
like it could be me, and it could've been
thirty years ago. In fact, I'm pretty sure
it was.

My dad's face buckled
as if he'd been gut-punched
back when I'd gathered nerve
enough to announce my own
big news. He knew what I know now.
So what could he do but nod, pat my
shoulder, force a smile?

Birdie snags the waitress to question
this or that about the bill. Silly,
but I hold my breath to listen
how the topic moves closer to painfully
obvious. Both Birdie and Wanda fidget
in the bottom of their handbags
pretending they can't remember something
they've just remembered again
and then forgot. *Look Hon*, Birdie
says without looking up, *I want you
to have this*. It's a wad. Maybe
forty bucks. Wanda does the same.

Out-of-state plates zoom past
like nothing happens here. And I grin
through two eggs and toast. Savor
the coffee, every next swallow.
Tally comes to five seventy-five.
I doubt there's much more than that in my pocket,
but count on it . . . I leave it all.

Flying Toad

Plastic bracelet signifies
unescorted minor. Fidgety
pre-teen assigned
to the seat beside me. Shuttled
twixt Dad's new life,
Mom and her boyfriend back home.
Up in the air.

I shake my head
how the world's changed. The kid
flips open his lap-top. Splats
aliens, as a rap rift thumps
in his headphones. Shouts
at me like I can't hear.

And just when I'm pushed
at the edge of humanity's collapse,
the kid elbows me
to confess he's smuggled
contraband. A gift
for his best buddy in school.
(*Wanna see?*)

Digs in a hidden duffle.
Keeps a sharp eye
on the steward's back, turned. Extracts
a tattered shoebox, holes punched
top and sides.

It's a big one, he says.
Named Lumpy.

How He Cut Himself Shaving

Remember the wind as it rippled
over backwater brackish with one more August
lost in the last days of boy growing to man.
Remember the aspen leaves' tremble as they woke
so slowly to that breeze. The chill
up your spine clothed in naked bronze.
Your bare feet planted in muck to your knees.

Then to balance—part outside the surface, part below—
so that inside your flesh reflected, fish teemed
in knotted roots of the green world's desire
to bloom. And to know nothing
of how it would come to pass one lifetime removed
from where likely by now that slough was bulldozed
into tract homes and acres paved with the inevitable
improvements. And never to suspect

that simple whisper of breeze hinted
at the fury of currents burning spring to summer, summer
to fall. And the first breath of the opposite
sex inhaled that year at school.
The next year and the next and next.
The waters of love-making. Waters of the womb
breaking between the clean sheets that night
your wife came due and once more the boy in you
walked into the warm-blooded wash
of that sunlit muddy slough.

And never to have shuddered
suddenly out of a long sleep this morning
roused by the loud alarm
of hungry children.
And never to have left a place.
Never to have come back facing yourself lathered,
still shaving so thoughtlessly and innocently
out of control. To feel that wind.
Listen again to the aspen.
To stare. How the ripples grow and go.

Learning to Dance

Three bucks cover charge, five per couple,
Saturday night at the Eagle's Club downtown Kalispell.
Grandmothers of the Ladies' Auxiliary
mind a cash box at the door. *Good to go,* one nods to me.
Hope you and your Mrs. kick up some dust.

But the dance floor's spotless, shines
like a school gymnasium, the hall lit like junior prom,
a corner bandstand enshrined with twinkle lights,
and a galaxy of stars—the regulars—orbit
arm-in-arm, a cowboy two-step, skirts awhirl.

First we sit safe at a table out of view, nurse
margaritas, applaud the three weathered
calf ropers with guitars, silver haired rodeo queen
still in Wranglers, twanging songs all the geezers
and gussied-up ranch wives know to sing along.

We're not young as once, either. Our brood
out cruising Main with dates of their own,
and we're confused what we do without the need
to entertain them. Puzzle over which tunes
call for what step and which look almost easy,

like something we could try. And we do
muster the nerve to get up and slow dance,
shuffle like embraced mannequins, glance at the others
who've discovered how to sway with the rhythm
and move along. We laugh and forgive

our stumbles, one skill that's brought us this far.
And causes strangers to smile as we brave a waltz.
You're mouthing the count, my wife whispers. I blush,
clamp my jaw and concentrate. Watch our feet
align themselves, step again toward something new.

Sin and Salvation

In the kitchen she opens
and closes drawers, thumbs
overlapped stacks of what she's
clipped and tucked away. Sleuths
loose newspapers, notes, old mail.
She's just now forgotten what she'd
once remembered she'd filed,
something she wants me to see.
Vows again to straighten this mess.

It's an article she lifted
at her dentist's office last time
he put her through "So much pain,"
she says, "I wished I was dead."
It's an essay concerning the ever-
after, people who've been there
and come back. The great white
light, a whole life flashes fast-forward,
events reenacted long forgot.

"But no judgment against nobody,"
she tells me. And that's the point.
The good and bad merged.
Now she rips into boxes
of handwritten scraps, on her knees
in the bedroom nearby. Yells
to keep her conversation afloat.

Darn, she so badly wants me to read
exactly how the author told it. Says
she was so mad at the dentist,
she stole the whole magazine.
Stuck it under her housecoat. Tore
from it these couple important pages.
Burned the rest to cover her trail.

Together

She's a bit puffy-eyed, but smiles
as if whatever went on last night
was worth it. He's even less well
put together: rumpled western shirt,
pearl snaps on the cuffs unbuttoned,
fingers combing his dark curls
with one free hand, his other locked
tight as a rawhide knot with hers.

They tumble into the farthest corner
seats, waiting to board the plane.
We give them the whole row,
watch him rest his chin
on her head nestled into his shoulder.
And listen as they share a cup
of the same coffee we couldn't stomach
—from the same machine—passing it
eyes closed after each sip
as if nothing has ever tasted so good.

We guess—my wife and I—they're
new at this much love, hovering
at that high pitch of ecstasy, world
be damned to go on alone without them.
Both of us know too well what's to come.
She's saying goodbye now, whispering it
when they stand and lean into each other,
paused as if in prayer. My wife
lays her hand over mine.
We say one too.

Go Fish

I visited my father
week-to-week
in a twelve-by-twelve room
supervised
by a woman who sat
in a corner
reading a book
to make sure
my dad
didn't take me away.

In the summer
there was no air conditioning.
In the winter
there was no Christmas tree.
Just a table,
a lamp.
Sometimes the lady
brought a deck of cards.
My dad taught me
Go Fish.

When our time ended,
Mom was waiting
by the door
to take me home.
I'd wave goodbye
to Dad. He smiled.
Shut the door.
I thought he lived there.

Someday you can choose
where you'll live, Dad
used to say.
With him, with her.
All I had to do was close my eyes
and point. Pick a card.
Go Fish.

Remembering a Visit to My Father

I saluted the cheap white rock that bears his name,
Marble medal with moss-stained epaulets
Won in horror and blood on some South Sea island
Long before I was born.

We both wore different uniforms once.

Mine was green piping on soft gray wool.
Rounding the bases breathlessly on boyhood legs,
I saw my father coaching third, like always,
Waving me home, eyes locked on the outfielder's
Long throw. "Don't look at the ball—keep going!"

Sentenced him, decades after, to solitary life
In that sanitary room with soft walls.
Sick. Now dead. Lying there
Under a cold quilt of newly fallen leaves.

I lowered my salute. Shivered
In the brittle breeze of oncoming winter,
Still rounding third toward home.

Pony, Montana

I came here to get away, finish the book,
hole up in the ramshackle, rented sight unseen.
Plastic flowers and saggy bed. Hard living
killed the owner last year, his pipe on a shelf.
East of Butte, you get off at Cardwell, head south.
I backed in so they wouldn't see my rainbow.

A short guy named Tecumseh called it Pony.
He came for gold. Morris State Bank still stands
before Hollowtop, bricks and plywood windows
alone against white mountains in June,
empty of the assay. The Tobacco Roots
run west of this town, now in its third boom.

At the park where my cell phone came in range,
I barely noticed the kid near the fire pit,
analogue roaming and voice messages.
He scuffed by, under his cap a long look
pleaded his need, a reckless stare ignored.
Fading in and out, I strained to catch words.

First they took the lode with pick axe. Pony grew.
On the hillside, the school juts up. I saw him
zigzag through gravel framed by red brick,
out of place, picking up rocks, looking back at me,
the stranger twice his age focused on a phone.
Unreachable. Cyanide brought the second

rush, slant-roof Victorians still howling
when thunder haunts the night and frantic bats
swoop down to raise adrenalin. Not until
I rocked in the garden watching aspens shuffle
did I see the bale in those eyes, unable
to stop the flapping plastic I masked up

to keep those trapped bats out. That black figure
chasing me down the stairs. The locked door.
Bad dreams veering off walls. I am scared here
in the new tourist town with its double-wide
post office. Its drunk bar. Scared someone might
find out. Come get me for what I saw in him.

Agnes

--for Agnes Vanderberg

We hide-tan here at Agency Creek
and at Valley Creek. Hard work
that lets your mind go as you wait
for the rest of your life. Soft hide,
so soft wind blows like cloth.
Hair white with hide.

She, Agnes, watches and lets us know in old
Salish tongue. Word for scraper that I
remember now. So hard.   So to the point.

Why did I learn how to write? Why did I want to?
Is it worth the loss of your world going away?

Bad Wine

You can love a dying Indian,
But when he drinks bad wine
And breaks your best glass
You give him to the wind.

Put Šey	**That Is All**
Steṁ a spuʔus?	What's in your heart?
Steṁ ɬu smimiʔʔ	What's the news?
Sqlqėlixʷ	Indian People
Sqlqėlixʷ	Indian People
Spq̇niʔ	Sun
Spq̇niʔ	Moon
Kʷk̇ʷusṁ	Stars
Q es čɬacxeneɬs	Watch over us
Qe uɬ scnk̇ʷeṅ	We are the chosen people
Qe uɬ scnk̇ʷeṅ	We are the chosen people
Ci q̇ʷelm	We hear
Iše qe qe sewneʔ	Our
Tqe sq̇spsq̇ʷelm	Ancient Songs
Šeẏ ɬu qe sxʷlšitusm	That is our guide
Iše qe nk̇ʷṅk̇ʷṅem	We sing these songs
Ẏe t q̇ʷelm še qe npiyels	And we are happy
X̣est	Good
Put šeẏ.	That is all.

Translated by: Victor Charlo, April Charlo, and Sophie Mays

Last Day

Suppose you were fey enough
to realize this day
was your last.
What would you do with it?

Would you open your eyes
and really see
the beauty of the world
about you?

Wouldn't you want to cry out
to anyone who would listen,
Stop your mad rushing about!
False dreams!

Enjoy the wonders you possess.
Look up! Look up
at the sun-sparkled sky.
At the clouds. A bird flying by.

See green grass,
the trees, the flowers.
Breathe in the sweet air.
Just take a walk.

Pat a dog.
Hear the melody of children's laughter.
Talk to a friend. Listen
to music. Read a poem.

Look around and really see
all the world you pass so quickly by.
Think about the sweet smell of lilacs
in rain-washed air.

Remember the smell of baking bread.
Of coffee and frying ham
by a campfire.
The wind in the pines.

Sit beside
the person you love.
Watch the sunset.
Crimson, purple, gold.

October Lament

We'll go to the woods no more.
The flowers are all gone.
The blossomed meadows
where once the muses danced
in fairy moonlight,
all bare and brown.

This year draws in its days.
Twilight soon.
And we'll to the Park no more.
Its elusive summer magic gone.
No more, no more this year,
wandering through shaded fragrant silence.

We'll miss the muted sound of waterfall.
The sudden sight of deer
on a leafy canopied trail.
A soft bird song.
The musical wind
playing melodies on the golden aspen leaves.

The sparkling sky.
The tumbled clouds.
No more to the wild high places
where the wind roars.
The mystical distances.

So lovely. So lovely all.
Lots of memories to share
with beloved companions.
Now summer's gone.
No more for us this year.

The Lost Meadow

I remembered a high mountain meadow
carpeted with flowers, lupine and paintbrush.
A fragrant rainbow, circled by mountains
near Preston Park.

Tall bear grass lined the trail
through the forest. Past
rushing streams.

I hunted that meadow, ever climbing
last Sunday afternoon. Hunting
what I'd loved so many years ago.

One hiking partner
gave up after two miles and lay down
under the pines.
I gave up
after another mile. Sat on a log.
Sat alone in the wilderness.
Jagged peaks all about me.
Thoughts of bears.
Total silence.

Then went on, and finally found the place
I'd longed for. But
not the flowered meadow. The years
had turned my meadow
into a seedling forest.

My tears blurred it all.
All this wild beauty. The world
is old enough
to break my heart.

Larson's Holstein Bull

Death waits inside us for a door to open.

Death is patient as a dead cat.

Death is a doorknob made of flesh.

Death is that angelic farm girl

gored by the bull on her way home

from school, crossing the pasture

for a shortcut. In the seventh grade

she couldn't read or write. She wasn't a virgin.

She was "simple minded," we all said.

It was May, a time of lilacs and shooting stars.

She's lived in my memory for sixty years.

Death steals everything except our stories.

Stubble

He collapses like a spine-shot buck
miles short of the fishing hole
we've trudged toward
one too many years.

I kneel,
nestle his grey head closer
than he held me
in Mother's old photographs.

He taught me
how to sharpen a knife
and the pitch of an idling engine.
My lips
had never touched him.

His stubble tastes
bitter
where puffing spilled Day's Work chew.
His chest rises
with my soft breath.

A Day When Ribbons and Medals Had Meaning

(for my niece, Renie Coles)

You taught me how to lead.
You were an athlete in the Olympics
that became special to me
when you dashed in the right direction
of 100 wandering yards of play.

You were so far ahead
of your friends you sensed
something was missing. So...
you stopped
in the two most important tracks
left in the grass that day.
You turned to your friends because
they were your friends,
and you waved and cheered
them closer as they pumped and huffed
as fast as each was able.
And you all finished in the plenty
of time.

Cuffs

In the mirror
the deputy's satanic eyes
judge me guilty
of schizophrenia.

I wring my hands white
and turn my burned stare
through the heavily
screened windows
of the patrol car.

Fragmented ranches
and towns
reel me closer
to the State Hospital. It lurks
just beyond the carved leap
of the horizon.

For something to do
and freedom
my hands try
to squirm from metal cuffs. Impossible

to piece together this grim disease
and the State's right to refuse
my right to die.

My bladder aches from the long drive.
The deputy says one
more hour.

Winter Kills: The Paschal Mystery

(Two horses were found during the spring
thaw at Lubec, where Glacier Park and
Blackfeet land meet.)

The springtime foal bucks in raven clothes.
Black scavengers feed, framed in ribs and skin.
The naked planet lies exposed.

Indian horses. Blood, thorned like a Blackfeet rose.
Ash-gray bones, emptied by winter wind.
The springtime foal bucks in raven clothes.

Winter kills. Named, yet nothing disclosed.
A pale moon coyote howls the evening thin.
The naked planet lies exposed.

Ravens, heavy-bellied against tomorrow, doze.
Prairie night crouches, jaw rimmed.
The springtime foal bucks in raven clothes.

Range horses, their long-grass days now frozen
To the Blackfeet plain, where the feral snow spins.
The naked planet lies exposed.

Tell horses that ice-snuffed springs are mere repose.
Explain that the stalking night is only kin.
The springtime foal bucks in raven clothes.
The naked planet lies exposed.

Loki/ The Messenger

I brake. Turn around.
Park by the side of the road.
Walk out to remove a turtle
that grows like an island
from the center, yellow line.
His shell is cracked.
A gaping wound, looking
like a great earthquake
had pulled the two halves—
the continent of its shell—apart.
And, in all that dark space,
thin lines of muscles
and a beating heart.
I have never seen
a beating heart. I take him
home. At home

he sits in a shoe box lid,
on the kitchen table, in a slow circle
of his own spreading blood. I look
into the strange, yellow stripes
of his eyes. Let his clear, hooked claws
rest on my fingers. Brew up a tea
of slippery elm, golden seal and yarrow,
that I soak the bandage
to wrap him in.
I talk to him. Tell him
that I know no turtle medicine.
He talks to me. Tells me
that he is a messenger. That my shell
is cracked. My heart exposed.
My heart beating.
How I've outgrown
this self-imposed limitation
of form.

Mothers Day, 1996

On Mothers Day, we ride
out in your pickup, to bring home
an over-flowing load
of manure. Your truck buckles
under the weight. The tires
almost go flat. Driving
through town, I feel
all eyes upon us, staring,
like Mothers Day and manure
somehow relate, somehow
intertwine. At Montana Market,
you come into the store
and buy me a broom, asking
my opinion. At the check-out counter,
we joke about how you know
how to satisfy a woman, you know
what a woman
really needs. We joke
and I turn my head away
to write out a check, smiling
unevenly.

                    I really do need
a new broom.

At home, you unload the manure
into the garden,
while I carry the groceries
into the house. Carry
in my new broom
like some prized treasure.
There is dirt on the floor, half-swept
piles. The daughter
sits reading
on the couch. There is
so much to do, so much
that I don't ask for, so much
I have never asked for.
I put the groceries away, pick
up the broom, begin
another year of sweeping.

Morning

Each morning, wrapped
in my red coat, I weave
my way through the tumbling heads
of yarrow, past purple asters
and snowberry, past Oregon grapes,
now long past flowering, to the edge
of the swamp, where I stop
and say my prayers. Cattails
explode in front of me, waving fingers
of shadow and light. Ghost clouds
of mist rise from the lake
edged in by the dark, climbing forest
beyond. It is just me
and the sun
who peers upon this morning world
shrouded in bird song and mosquito wings.
Just me standing there locked
inside my fears, trying desperately
to get out. "Spirit,"
I call out abandoning myself
to the moment. "I am
standing here at the edge
of the swamp, at the edge
of my world, praying for vision
and for trust. Help me to believe
in my husband's healing. Help me
to walk my heart path
upon this earth. To see
my heart path upon this earth." I hold
tobacco in my right hand, cornmeal
in my left. My hands are open,
raised toward the sky. My prayers
unfold around me, taking in
the fullness, the ripeness
of all life. "Bless the four leggeds,
the creepy crawly people, the finned
ones, the tall standing people,
the short standing people, the rocks
and the stars. Bless all
the two leggeds, all of those
who mourn or are angry
or feel pain. Bless the leaders
of the world, so they may come
into right relationship. Bless
the Earth Mother, herself, so she too

may heal. Bless my family
and me. Keep us safe
through this day." I lower my hands,
crumble the tobacco onto the earth, watch
as it takes root among the silver weed,
it too now past flowering. "I remember,
my oneness with all life," I say,
then unfold my left hand, releasing
cornmeal in a fine, blue stream.
"With this cornmeal," I pray,
"I remember that life gives away
so I may live. Ho."
It is done. Done. I take
a deep breath in. Wipe my hands
against my skirt. Bow low
to the horizon, then turn
to face my day.

Drilling the Well

The sad horse plods
a round path, crosses
its beginning again and again.
The driller rolls casing
across the yard. Tattoos ripple.
Veins cord along his arms.
He measures the day in cigarettes
and swallows from the bottle
in his truck. When I pass him
as I do my chores, his eyes
stare overlong until he turns
and slaps the horse's rump.
My father comes to sit with him
along the north side of the house,
listens to Navy stories
of native girls and nights in port,
of storms at sea and German submarines.
I wash dishes at the sink, unconscious
of the motion of my hands.
Through the window, I watch
the horse trace its mindless circle.

Rivers of Horses

All you real human beings, listen.
This is the story of the coming of the horse.
Out of a dream they came to the Crow,
Sioux, Cheyenne, and Arapaho,
through the north plains and mountains,
grazed around the wolf and buffalo.
Flowing herds of horses.
Rich flowing herds of horses.
Rivers of horses.
Up and down these coulees and draws
from the Rio Grande and the Platte
and the Powder River flow herds
of this mystic pony.

Of this mystic pony.
Tapping willow stick, I can still hear.
I can hear my grandfather tapping Painted Black
with a willow stick. A long time ago
my grandfather, Owns-Painted-Horse,
behind him I sat
on his horse Painted Black.
I hugged him lightly,
leaned the side of my face
gently against his back.
"These horses have a soul.
Do them good. And respect them.
Talk good to them, and they know.
They talk to each other.
When you talk good to the horses' spirit,
they will come to you and you will be
lucky with horses if your heart is good."
Said my grandfather, Owns-Painted-Horse.

At the edge of my vision, something flew by
and returned into my feeling.
You're so far away from me, Grandfather,
as I stare into the twinkle and glitter
of snowflakes in the wind.
Great horses made great warriors.
Atop a fast running buffalo horse,
he could stick an arrow behind the last rib,
deep into the heart
of a fast running buffalo. And the hides
on his lodge reflected the quality of horses he rode.
The warrior's people ate the best of meat,

packed into camp on his many horses.
His prized war-horse tied to his thigh
as it grazed outside the lodge by night.
Great horses made great warriors.
Carried him to strike the grand coup,
rush up and touch the enemy
while he was still alive.
Many feathers of grand coup,
and return with many horses,
a long-tailed war bonnet.
Great horses made great warriors.
The next-best coup
was to enter the enemy camp by night
and cut the rawhide rope knotted
to the sleeping enemy warrior.
Drive the un-tethered war-horses home.

From a dream he was given his
white sorrel medicine horse paint,
in the shadow of Shining Mountains,
in the Moon of First Thunder.
Astride his medicine horse paint,
swoop up and steal a beautiful woman
from lodges different than his own.
Carry the beautiful woman home.
His song they would sing,
as he danced the Scalp Dance, Victory Dance.
As he gave away his best horses,
fast running horses, to spread
the good fortune among his people.
He was close to the horse's spirit.
And he could lead a war party.
Become Chief, the man that is good.
Because the Maker blessed him with great horses,
so he had someone to lean his back against.
The great horse made the great warrior.

I remember pulling strands of sinew thread
to run through my mouth, pinch one end
then roll-twist the braid down the outside
of my right thigh, in the late snowy night.
I got up to poke the fire. This story
from Grandmother Everything-She-Joins:
"Horses to show love. The brother
would give his new brother-in-law a good horse
to show respect for his sister. A girl's parents
would give ten good horses
to marry their daughter to a great warrior.

But a man who is not a man
would give horses to a girl's parents
for her hand in marriage. The great warrior
had many horses. And many wives.
That's how it was.
The children of a respectable family
would ride Appaloosa horses
with no tails. Old folks' horses and kids' horses
wore squared-off tails. That's how it was.
These great horses made great people.
Bird Horse. Horse on the Other Side.
Medicine Tail. Pretty Paint. Rides-the-Horse.
Takes-the-Horse. Horse Herder. Spotted Horse.
Brings-Home-Many-Geldings. Has-Lots-of-Colts.
Lucky-With-His-Horse. Always-Rides-Horses.
Grey Horse Rider. Sorrel Horse. Buckskin Horse.
Black Horse Rider. Lead Horse Rider.
These are the names. Great horses.
Great people.

Then came the day my father's horses
were killed by the Bureau of Indian Affairs
and sell-out Indians for 25 cents an ear.
And they killed coyote and magpie.
Before that, the buffalo and wolf were gone.
The sheep and spotted buffalo
ate the buffalo grass . . . .
Don't you shed a tear for the horses
for they replaced a human being's life,"
said my grandmother, Everything-She-Joins,
Florence Medicine Tail Real Bird,
"but that day, I made my tears drop
when they killed all the horses.
That was a bad day. My heart was bad.
If these were the days when the lodges used to move
my heart would be extremely good."

Painted-Black-Horse-Rider, Spirit-Horse-Rider,
Protector, Defender of the Crow
who still ride the prairies and the mountains,
I have always been told about you.
So now I offer this prayer. A river
of prayer for the horses.
Rivers of horses. I offer you,
Painted-Black-Horse-Rider,
a river of smoke
from my sacred pipe.
For many good tomorrows.

Tripwire

When Jones tripped

the wire that exploded

the buried 500-pound bomb,

he was blown up

and apart.

Jones ceased to exist

except for one combat boot

pointing down the jungle trail

and a fine, red mist

settling,

settling . . .

Evening Pruning

My father and I prune dead branches from the apricot trees.
Brittle winter-kill twigs crack beneath our feet.
Fruitless limbs arch through deepening sky.
He speculates aloud which cold snap has set us now to work.
We shuffle between the trees, our necks craned,
Avoiding each other's eyes.

My sisters take possession of mother's kitchen,
Empty closets of her clothes,
Sift through a lifetime of scarves, mended nightgowns,
Finding slips of paper with quotations from her reading,
Grocery lists in the pockets of her coats,
Pigtails lopped cleanly from their heads,
Tied in ribbons thirty five years ago.

Even after she has them pitted and halved,
Mother holds the paring knife ready in her hand,
holding out three apricot halves.
We hesitate with the primal harvest whole in our hands.
She eats her share unhesitatingly.
Dad, Karen, and I watch her break into giggles
the yield and the ceremony too much to contain,
the juice finding the corners of her mouth.

In the half light, the pruning done, my father confesses:
You know, I still have her ashes in the house.
Would it be good to spread them behind the garden
Where the deer bed down?
At least for this moment inside his worried eyes
I give her back to the trees.

October in Montana

Gathering yearlings,
this cow horse and I, stumble-footed
down a dry creek bed.
Crows squawking overhead.
The horse stalls, ears flicker
toward campfire banter.
Hunters.

Hunters are a disquieting prospect
when you're riding
a reddish-brown horse.
Hunters of indeterminate merit
have been known to shoot
anything in sight
that has four legs.
Many a Montana outfitter can tell
that tale.

They were drinking
pungent cowboy coffee.
The bitter perfume of scorched beans
rattled out of their pot.
They'd gathered around their meal,
backs to my direction.

I coughed loudly
and sang a bit of song about
"going to the chapel,"
as I rode up the side of the hill
and through the brush.

I sang like no elk knows how.

Harlem Montana: Just Off the Reservation

We need no runners here. Booze is law
and all the Indians drink in the best tavern.
Money is free if you're poor enough.
Disgusted, busted whites are running
for office in this town. The constable,
a local farmer, plants the jail with wild
raven-haired stiffs who beg just one more drink.
One drunk, a former Methodist, becomes a saint
in the Indian church, bugs the plaster man
on the cross with snakes. If his knuckles broke,
he'd see those women wail the graves goodbye.

Goodbye, goodbye, Harlem on the rocks,
so bigoted, you forgot the latest joke,
so lonely, you'd welcome a battalion of Turks
to rule your women. What you don't know,
what you will never know or want to learn—
Turks aren't white. Turks are olive, unwelcome
alive in any town. Turks would use
your one dingy park to declare a need for loot.
Turks say bring it, step quickly, lay down and dead.

Here we are when men were nice. This photo, hung
in the New England Hotel lobby, shows them nicer
than pie, agreeable to the warring bands of redskins
who demanded protection money for the price of food.
Now, only Hutterites out north are nice. We hate
them. They are tough and their crops are always good.
We accuse them of idiocy and believe their belief all wrong.

Harlem, your hotel is overnamed, your children
are raggedy-assed but you go on, survive
the bad food from the two cafes and peddle
your hate for the wild who bring you money.
When you die, if you die, will you remember
the three young bucks who shot the grocery store up,
locked themselves in and cried for days, we're rich
help us, oh God, we're rich.

Why I Didn't Go to Delphi

My feet taste funny
in this light.
Flowers tell me nothing.
Was it all a dream,
a morning made by birds
sailing to Glyfada, dodging
caiques, red breezes
north from Africa?

Nikos drove that wet sea
wild with explanations
of demotic songs, Count Basie,
goat feet tender to the cliff.

I believed that slapstick chin,
old gestures of disdain,
older gestures of the knife
slicing off that final breath
of fifteen day old lambs.

The butcher looked up,
startled. His mother
brought a basin of water.
Reflected off Hymettus,
the sea changed to asphodel.
Children who could not speak
spoke, and that sad oracle
wild with premonition,
for the seventh time
explained the origin of death.

Photo by Greg Keeler

Greg Keeler

Worth Bombing For

Yesterday some guy nicks my wife's
car with his SUV in the Target parking
lot then starts screaming as if his life
were ending. Judy thinks the guy is joking,
but he isn't. He's scratched his giant box
which he's only owned for thirteen days.
"It's your fault," he screams, then he talks
to the cops on his cell. While they're on their way
he sees her bumper sticker, IMPERIALISM
A WAY OF LIFE WORTH BOMBING FOR,
and basically calls her a traitor. It isn't
long before the cops come. "Is there anything more?"
they ask when they see it's not life or death.
"Yeah," says my wife. "He tried to sell me meth."

Tiny Times of Zen

Some people split themselves in two: a life
for home, a life for away; a life for night,
a life for day; a life for friends, a life
for those who never had a friend. What might
their own lives be like, speeding back and forth
between the lives of others, a tremendous sense
of importance driving them toward the North
of success, toward the South of love? The dense
air within their cars, the tiny times
of Zen they don't even recognize
as the present, eating away their hearts. The crimes
multiply as they stare at their watches, the lies
they tell themselves to separate their lives,
butchering their souls with secret knives.

Philipsburg '94

(for Judy)

You came here Sunday, not on a whim
but more or less out of desperation.
We couldn't kiss or even touch
like years before. My life had broken down,
and I was pulling yours down with me.
So sick you had nowhere else to go,
you walked the streets with me in pain,
my hormones pulling us along like a mad dog,
past the shops and candy store struggling
to make the town quaint for us and
two or three other couples with kids,
which only reminded you that ours
were grown and gone. I'd tried to leave you
too—not for jazz, booze, or Butte—just the blonde
I thought the world would never let me have
but did. Almost fifty, I thought
I could accelerate my life, but I couldn't
leave you, so you had lain in a ball
on pillows in the back of our Camry,
trying to resurrect the life we'd known.
Refurbished Victoriana the local mine had built
before the Silver Bill's repeal shined like new
in sun so bright we couldn't see the hills
or cattle we knew were grazing there.
You asked if this was now my life,
our twenty years together burning
out your eyes. Or is this, you asked,
defeat, and I followed your gaze
down a street of light and shadow
empty and clear as a Hopper painting.
I told you no, but you knew I was
talking to myself. We had come to see
some actor friends in a farce
at the summer theater, but at curtain time,
all the seats were empty, and we left
before they saw us. We felt so wrecked,
we were surprised when the car started
and again when the kid at the convenience store
accepted our credit card. On our way out,
the sun hit your hair in such a way
that I could barely see the road.

What Makes A Patriot?

Mr. Armchair General. Colonel Couch Potato.
CNN. Fox News.
What makes a Patriot?
To die? To be a name on a monument?
Would you listen to me then?

I stood in front of your courthouse.
Sign in my hand: Are Your Children Collateral Damage?
Wearing a green field jacket. Not good camouflage in the snow.
Government issue.
I did my time. Served my sentence.
Why did you blow your horn,
yell at me? *Get a job, you fucking hippie.*

For you, young man in your SUV, once
I worked for you. Took an oath
to uphold and defend. Back then
you were playing in a remote sandbox.
While I rode a 62 ton tank. Steel tracks in the sand.
My lungs full of gunpowder and diesel.
You were home eating Cap'n Crunch
while I sat in a foxhole in the rain.
Eating cold green eggs. Overhead
red tracers seeking vengeance.

My breech is now closed.
No more canisters of death.
(By the way, have you witnessed death?
Lye smells? Plastic zippered body bags?
72 hours, then the intestines rupture.
Some still have purple hard-ons.)
But there you were in Aunt Sally's backyard raking leaves for 5 dollars.
I raked up your enemy.
My killing days are over.
Now I am everything wrong with your America.

Flying Kite

Self assured.
Pulled taut.
Rising arrogantly on
full support of winds.

Moments of unsteadiness.
Riding out the gusts.
Challenging the strength
of the strings attached.

The struggle and resistance
gives passage to the altitudes,
a higher perspective.
Flight.

Big Open

(Ingomar, Montana)

I'm pregnancy testing a thousand
mother cows
under a warm sweet wind. Spilt milk
clouds. Green grass
in November. Ringtailed hawks
perch over the emptiness
on cottonwoods of Little McGinnis Creek
waiting for death that will not come.

Antelope and mule deer graze
unafraid, knowing
we have no rifles.

I give the late pregnancies another chance,
let them stay on
another year. Hoping
winter forgives them.
And me.

Stealing Fish

In the mountains
lie vistas
so holy

I imagine
myself in the
Garden of Eden

as Brueghel painted
the scene before
Adam and Eve

devoured the fruit
of their innocence; imagine
myself down the slope to the left

where the stream
disappears into a
woodland shading

crystal pools where
the first brook trout
rise to pale morning

duns. Still naked
casting a fly
through the mist

stealing fish from God.

Monk With A Cello

My friend hung a photo
on his bathroom wall:
a bearded monk
playing a cello.
The monk lives at home
with his loneliness.
As if the exquisite pain
of his solitude
were as perfect
as his mournful song
no one hears.

Tall In The Sidesaddle

Sidesaddle riding once was a must
For a lady in long-layered skirt.
With knee fitted over a cradling hook,
She mostly endured till it hurt.

In the East she was expert at riding to hounds
In habit and black derby hat;
A groom helped her mount with his hand on her rump.
(Of course *she* could never say that!)

If ever she tried to ride astride
There were gasps and glances askance;
In order to do so in practical garb,
She would have to wear—*masculine* PANTS!

But then she went west where the living was rough
To see what the real cowboys do.
To ride like a pretzel was painful and tough,
And twisted her backbone in two.

So she hiked up her skirts and piled on her bronc—
Put a leg on each side of her saddle.
With yippie ki yi she went searching the range
For cattle—*astraddle* her saddle.

History fails to mention her name,
This woman who helped win the West.
Though small, she was tall when she got on her horse,
And she rode and she roped with the best.

First Chore

(for Brooke)

The girl sobs, crouched
inside the barn door
opened wide on winter,
an eight year old crying in stereo
across the barn yard to where
the cats wail too. Lambs bleat
a sympathetic chorus
in the far corner of the shed.
Three horses look up from their feeding.
She hunches on knees
now darkened by tears
shoveling down
from two heaving shoulders.
All in response to a chore assigned.
To sweep up the loose straw
into one meticulous
mound. Nothing has been done.
The broom leans against
the closed stall door
as she continues to cry,
to cry even harder, against
the way the world wants her.

Finley Creek

March. I'm back in Arlee, Montana.
Watching the ice break in Finley Creek.
Smelling the sweet, bitterness of dead leaves,
sodden turf, crisp water.

I'm drawn here
awkward, uneasy,
heavy longing in my chest
as spring nudges sluggish winter
and low-leaden fog
drifts ponderously toward midday.

I hear my mother's voice calling me
back to parsnips and horseradish
buried in cold ground.
Harvested to our table.
Her shining face.

Rooted in spongy earth,
shadows of rainbow
dart through green weed.
I fish the seven holes of Finley Creek
and pull them out,
one by one,
like shimmering dreams.

Cars in The River

Like wet roads the cars can't travel
the river throws them off,
now grounded, some half buried
in the cutbank, beached whales.
Soaring silver fins, toothy catfish
grills. Sun-filled quiet
green water lounging in the back seat.

Now a fat dark Merc cools
in the shady flow, submerged to the dash.
Roll-overs and smash-ups.
Pushed through the pasture above,
rolled over the edge. Current breakers.
Mountain run-off erosion control.
Drop Ma's old Caddy down there.
Ram the Dodge into them willows.

I've crawled into these river relics,
heard the trickle of murmur through the chassis.
Something dead. Something alive
in the way water filled the trunk
and trout swam around in it,
feeding on what falls from the sky.
Felt how these armored road-warriors
too shall pass. Like us.
Imperials, Victorias, Bel-airs
and Regals, all
made of things from this earth.

Photo by Roger Dunsmore

Ed Lahey

Moving

Moving is a burdensome task.
There are so many boxes
to be filled and opened, stuff
to be put away, carried to the
garbage chute.

Tina is a whiz, without her I
would be lost. Moving is like dying.
I am almost seventy. My time is nearing.
Thanatos means death in Greek.
There is clarity in death, stuff for the
garbage chute.

A wedding just went by outside
my window, horns honking, tin cans
tied to the wedding car. Life is moving.
We think we are going somewhere.
Some believe in eternal life.
I believe in the garbage chute.

What to throw out, what to save?
It costs money to move. It takes energy
and effort. One has to identify things.
Suicide is not the answer.
I have lost a pair of trousers
which I need if I am to continue.

I must go on, life demands it of me.
The cemetery can wait. Every man is
a lighthouse waiting for the ship to come in.
Tina will find my trousers
and I will pull them on one leg at a time.
Life is moving.

Tour De Force

A maple leaf
disentangles itself
from other leaves
in a timid maneuver

begun by the kiss

of the sun   then
stretches into shape
as large as a girl's hand.

Lazy water skippers
crisscross
teeming pools
tick tick tick tick.

Rainbow minnows
hesitate   nose to rock
tiny fingers
in the stream   cohere

waiting.

Lilies rustle
in a small breeze
and goldenrod bow
along the banks.

Listen.

Up the river   fast
the sound of a thousand
dragonflies.

Three feet above water
a blue-grey kingfisher

speeding . . .

The Blind Horses

The old man in the hospital bed
with his horny yellow foot
stuck through the stainless rails,
claimed that July night—the one he picked to die on—
he smelled sulfur on his gown.

When he was my age he worked the lower levels of the
Lex in a great underground corral, yoked iron tongue to
wagons filled with ruby silver and peacock copper rock,
flaked sweet hay to horses, shot the worn out.

Dozens of tramway horses hauled hard
against whippletrees—rubbed the timbered tunnels
clean—pulling down the cribbed-up drifts,
brass lanterns swinging, work bits in their teeth,
slick with mine damp and cold to the touch.

Dry stulls in the crosscut cave of that stone corral caught
fire in '98. The horses, tunnel-blind from lack of light,
burned up in the green flame that licked the lagging
black in the Lexington Mine.

I met his eyes cracked white
like a drunk's who hasn't had a drink in months.
He said he could hear hoofbeats ring
and click against the granite footwalls.
He complained of being cold. His nostrils flared:
"I hear them breathing, Ed."

Confederate Shacks

I snowshoed over wind falls,
and watched hawks circle
Confederate Gulch.
Now gray ghosts inhabit homesteads
and the pain of Southern deserters
dissolves into wood rust
beneath hawk shadow and the ache
of a hundred winters.

Each Northern drift crusts
thicker than Sherman's rubble.
Spirits in battered hats
haze whisker-frozen cattle
into wind-break barns.
They ditched the glory of the myth
and came from Southern hunger
to meet wind and canyon
far from managed battle.

Five miles up the gulch and tired,
the snow starched shack,
glazed remains of a weathered bunker
far from Shiloh.
Ice jarred the door case
but ricks of wood banked,
rot around the walls
to freeze in place.

What storm battalions could not do
I did by lifting up the latch.
Inside gone black in ash
of a decomposing room,
a shattered comb,
a picture of a woman,
yellow from back home,
a letter.

"Dearest…
        Forgive me…Daddy says…"
When I left I slammed the goddamn door.

Hawks in sun sail
echoes over monstrous tracks.
It makes no difference.
No smoke rises from dead shacks.

Gimp O'Leary's Iron Works

(for Big Ed)

You hear a lot of lies about O'Leary
but he could seal a crack in steel
no matter what the size.
His arc welder would strike
white fire and a bead
of blue-black rod would slide
along between cherry streaks,
and acrid smoke would curl away
to leave clean married steel,
not too frail, or buttered up
but straight and strong,
hard as mill forged rail.

Of course you might say,
"Don't use that example
as a metaphor for poetry.
Welding is a matter of utility."
And you'd be right. Still,
I remember the look on his face
when he'd lift his great helmet
and sneak up on the finished
job with his unprotected eyes.
It was always between him
and the piece of steel—
a struggle of molecules and will.

Often others would say to him,
"Damn good job" or some such thing.
If it was, he'd grin, and look again,
as if he thought the natural light
would show a flaw, or bridge
that didn't fuse—convinced, I guess,
that in his struggle with the steel
he could seldom really win.
He knew perfection could
conceal the wound
beneath the arc of his art.
I liked him for that.

Chew On, Chew On

If there is a God,
because there is a God
we were taught
judgment will be perfect,
but what is thought anyway?

Walking yesterday
along the Sorry River
my friend and I came upon a tree
felled by a beaver,
a big tree, by God.

It fell across
a cement retainer wall,
as though the fall was aimed
by a last resistance
in the toothy beaver's brain.

The beaver is not convinced
his work is inferior
to the Corps of Engineers
the City Fathers hire
to keep the river tame,
not convinced
his dams are less significant.

I love the beaver
and my old friend
who laughed like hell
in appreciation
figuring the beaver
might hear him, take heart
and chew on, right or wrong,
by God, chew on.

Birds of a Feather

(For Marylor)

A woman I love, my ex-wife
with our infant granddaughter
rounded an aisle
in the new Safeway
where we were shopping.

"There's a sparrow flying overhead,"

she said, when she saw me.
We both looked upwards.
I wanted so badly
to tell her something
she could cherish, so she
would know

that I love her, like her even,
more than I hate her, but all
I could think of was a bird
I once saw shredded
by an exhaust fan.

Feathers floating willy nilly.

She looked so fey
upon hearing my story, shyly,
so shyly, walking away,
pushing the stroller down
another aisle.

Leaving me again, again,
dead feathers gathering
about my feet.

Inside Her

"I'm in deep trouble,"
she said to him,
the first time in history
anyone had spoken of me.

The year 1936, Butte, Montana,
not far from here.
She was 18. He had
just come down the hill,
a shift in the Neversweat,
$2 a day on a widowmaker.

She bawled, then soft tears.
"What should we do?"
"This is a fine time to ask," he said
looking at his muddy brogans,
his face coal dark.

They fought and screamed
at one another, then a long
silence and she asked again, "Well?"
All the while I lay curled up
my heart beating in the darkness
inside her.

Poem For Daughters Who Garden

(To Naomi and Maia)

Today there are robins.

One struts across the patio,

still fat from jungle

bugs. My friend on the phone

has never seen them here, so

far from Connecticut or Montana.

I part the blind. Twenty at least

rest like plums in the gnarled hand

of a mulberry. They won't stay,

not here in this razored edge

of Chihuahuan desert. They've heard

the earthworms stir up north.

Their girth is fuel to see

them through the grainy ebb

of winter. In a month they'll land

in my daughter's yard, pick and peck

around islands of frozen dog prints,

cock their heads and listen

for movement underground. Her cats

will watch, eyes narrowed behind glass.

Oh look, she'll say, skin pale

as winter cream, spring is here.

And her daughter with the wild white hair

will raise her arms for Up

and say Where? Where? her tiny

memory filled with yellow jonquils.

Gypsy Son

The gypsy son hauls his ailing carcass across six hundred miles of winter road;
six hundred miles of snow-banked, black iced, two lane highway
over Roger's Pass past the Wolf Creek cut-off through Sun River,
with the usual time out for a sugared donut and a fuel-up in Vaughn.
A faltering middle-aged body keeps that black Grand Cherokee
doing its job through Loma, Chinook, and just east of Dotson
the gypsy catches a glimpse of his great-grandfather
between snow squalls, an old man not dressed for winter
working a big-boned black stud through a snow-choked gully,
long white hair blowing like tattered bed sheets in the wind.

The gypsy son cruises glassy-eyed into Glasgow beneath a purple
cloud-banked sky scalloped pink by the last of the sun behind him,
four hundred and fifty miles under his belt and still fighting the flu,
he staggers into a café bar and drops a shot of Knob Creek bourbon
into a cup of coffee, for god's sake, things are going to hell in eastern Montana
when the coffee is fresh-ground and the bar-keep with a Queens accent
hands you a cell-phone that announces you'd better not take a room,
that your father has been stroked into paralysis and blindness,
curled up in his bed like a crispy critter and going fast,
groping aimlessly with the only hand he's still got some use of.

One hundred and fifty more miles of iced up bridges and a right turn
off the high-line highway at Culbertson brings the gypsy son
across the Missouri and to the room where his father
is making a last stand, reaching out with that one good hand
as though pulling on a rope that's going to take him somewhere.
The son tells the father that he's dying, in case he doesn't know,
that it might be a good time to let it all go, all eighty-seven goddamn years
of not enough pasture, of a wife broken by hard work and too many deaths,
of a mother broken by a grandfather who broke everything he ever touched
including that section out south that never should have gone under the plow.

Requiem for Louie Z – 1994

Louie, 16, and his
two Vaseline-slick buddies. Him, the
"Boss," dirty sneakers kicked up on
our freshly-painted white porch rail, lounging
in our new Sears lawn-chair, ready
　　　　for anything. Next year he'd trade
　　　　his rusty, 5-buck bike for a motorcycle and chain. So
　　　　he claimed. His long soiled rooster neck thick
　　　　with muscle twisted my way: "We're
　　　　stayin.' Wanna do somethin' bout
it, fat boy?" Last week, age
46, Louie went away—cancer. That
long neck and maybe a million
Camels betrayed him. He went
the American way—the way of
　　　　lumps. Hope he still wore
　　　　those sneakers and that sneer, parked both
　　　　where they weren't wanted. Hope he kept
　　　　his long carved diseased neck twisted
　　　　in challenge: "Hey, you wanna
do
somethin'?"

Again, Grandpa

I could always smell
Grandpa's Chesterfields
coming through the open
transom above the door
to their room in the Ridpath Hotel
in Spokane, Washington.
And I got all excited because
me and Grandpa, we're like two

peanuts in a pod:
We both get in trouble with
Grandma a lot—and we both
love the Milwaukee Depot
and its rest'raunt with French
pancakes—and the freight trains
pulled by Little Joes
(those're the locomotives
named for the Emporer of Russia,

who's fightin' Nazis with us
in the war). And—we love
the Clark Fork River,
'specially where Petty Creek
runs in. That's where
we useta sit on the bank
and watch my dad catch
a Rainbow trout big
enough for all our dinner.

Next

Waiting wasn't a problem for him,
he'd brought something to read, yet sitting
there for almost an hour in the waiting room

at the proctologist's office, while
the badger in his ass huffed & scratched,
dug & growled (as it had for the last six months)

was enough to fan smoldering piles to flame,
prompt him to plan his wake & epitaph — maybe lift
a line from Carver or Plath.

Hours prior to the appointment,
he'd stood & stared, mesmerized by April rain,
a steady downpour all day:

noticed small buds bulging at the tips
of branches; puddles blooming into murky
ponds; & recalled the pure happiness

he'd felt the night before: lying there
wide awake after crawling back into bed
from his midnight trip to the toilet,

he slipped his arm around her,
pulled into her heat, felt his
heartbeats waltz her breath & thought:

Who cares what's next?
The prognosis is death — but tonight,
I'm the luckiest asshole alive.

a poem

is a memorial
in a way,
so today
i honor those

who've passed
before me
with this
short note

doctor Williams
might okay,
and bukowski surely
would salute

if say it
bought him a beer
and didn't insist
on parading us

this year
through blood
puddles & gunshots,
past uniforms

blowing smoke
about *what it takes*
to kill or die.
It takes everything:

the red wheelbarrow,
the white chickens,
the blue whores
glazed with rain.

(in memory of william carlos williams, charles
bukowski, & my old man on memorial day 2005)

The Weightless Spray Of A Perfect Dive

A passer-by tried to talk the youth
out of jumping, the twenty-something
year old sitting on the metal railing
of the bridge watching, along with others,
a resplendent, deepening, early June
crimson sunset. He had asked the passer-by
if he wouldn't meet him downstream
on the Caras Park side of the Clark Fork
thanking him for putting up with his socks
and t-shirt, boots and jacket, his wallet.
He said it was just months ago he had perfected
his swan dives off cliffs in Hawaii.

Skin showed through the tattered knees
of his Levis. He bore a tattoo on a forearm,
another across a shoulder. The tops
of his feet were tanned, too. Standing
on the lower railing, wedging his weight
against the top in the crooks of his knees,
he brushed his sun-highlighted hair aside
and in one continuous motion lofted
himself off and away from the bridge,
head thrown back, arms spread wide of his chest,
and in the blink of an eye, was gone.

His form held, his hands
linking together just as he knifed
into the icy peak-of-the-runoff
without as much as a splash.
The man with the belongings
ran down the stairs from the bridge
to the park shouting for help,
even wading out some distance
trying, if he could, to reach the diver.
Witnesses said the body surfaced
briefly but was motionless
in the murky current
then disappeared downstream.

His father, interviewed in his California home,
said he could see why his son loved it up there
in Montana. Around all that beautiful scenery
he was doing exactly what he wanted to do.
He complimented Search and Rescue for their effort
and kindnesses. Nine days after and five miles
downriver Glen Alan Morris Jr. was carried from the banks
of the Clark Fork where he had been spotted
in a log jam by a couple of kids
fishing at the head of Kelly Island.

Years later a father's feelings
for his son will continue to resonate.
Things his son might have said to himself
on the railing will give expression to themselves, too.
But there's little need to argue now
about how or why life sometimes unfolds
the way it does. People on a bridge
strolling under an engaging sunset
watched youthful exuberance
take a stab at something beautiful,
risking it all against rubble and stone.
They wondered if you could really plan
against things you can't see.
More difficult, they couldn't say whether
such a thing should never have happened.

Ninety Years

We sat together
while she pared
the apples—
the sun slipping through.
Granny Smiths and Macintosh.
She'd feed me a
slice and take
one herself as
we talked—
about what
I don't remember.

Later her daughter
baked the pie and
I came to
appreciate that what
had been passed
to her children
had now been
passed to me.

She knows she is dying
and says
she would just like
to know what day.
I left her with her daughter,
taking a piece
of pie wrapped in foil
in a brown paper bag.
I didn't know how
to say good-bye.

Cold Harbor

Crowd the coral chimneys of Nellie Sachs. Uphold!
The cranes will not land.
Was it Pound or T.S. betrayed "fuchsia d'or"?
How does one uphold bloodstained catalpa?

How does one uphold bloodstained catalpa
For conformity and quicksand on the Alexanderplatz
Sleeveless as a moonstone in Bremerhaven's shadow?
Once, he set us among princes like Bertolucci.

Once, he set us among princes like Bertolucci
On the Via Spoletto where lions roar;
One dare not uphold a paradise of honeyed misapprehension.
O Cold Harbor, count up the crow's nests in Canaan!

O Cold Harbor, count up the crow's nests in Canaan
At the center of an orange begonia moon
Where God comes dancing in the cool house
Of the craven and the mad
Nellie Sachs is waiting.

How does one uphold bloodstained catalpa?
Once, he set us among princes like Bertolucci.
O Cold Harbor, count up the crow's nests in Canaan!
Nellie Sachs is waiting.

Milk River Birthday

(for my mother)

Frozen streams curve
        thru stark brush
cold blue sky sprouts
        a cloud or two
the sun is almost warm
        a clatter of birds
        two dogs
I can't help but run
        groves of cottonwoods
        stand bare
along the river nothing
        rides the air
old men melt in my blood
        I pump a fresh
        feeling to my lungs
a wildness clears my heart
        a voice speaks
        in the frozen river
the trees wait.

Rumsey's 100 Stamp Mill

(1989—Montana's Centennial)

A curious surveyor stands alone
high on a crumbling foundation wall,
granite block in a mosaic terrace overlooking
the panoramic ruins of Rumsey's 100-stamp mill.
He's come to salvage the remains of the monumental
ambitions and labors that spill now into the silence
of this late summer evening.

Spread out below, a hillside cornucopia flows
into piles of tumbled granite stones
in their stillness stuck mid-bounce.
Rows of furnace firebrick arches
collapse into slides of raspy dust.
Wood timbers warp and splinter in piles.
Iron rods, bolts and nuts, twist in the debris.

Today in this year of Montana's centennial,
Rumsey's 100-stamp mill also celebrates
its century, the metes and bounds of boom and bust.
Abandoned years ago to Nature's conspiracy
of sun, wind, water—all relentlessly working
to dismantle the mill and reclaim the hillside.
History goes with that downward flow and floods away
into the willowy marsh of Fred Burr Creek below.

The Junkie Shuffle

From the codeine creep to a heroin nod
coming straight from a methamphetamine jitter bug,
he was jonesin' before he hit the door,
doing that infamous junkie shuffle.
The cry wheedle and whine, you know the one I mean,
the belly crawl, the one that comes when it's too late
and the insides have been sucked so dry
only the tortured eyes staring out from sunken sockets
resemble something too scary to feel sorry for.

Check it out, you got a disconnect notice on your reality here, brother,
you're coming in on a whole new frequency now.
The devil, you say, he just checked into the room next door,
the one with the hanging light bulb that dances naked with the girl upstairs
and the air conditioner that stinks of cigarettes and old carpet.
And then, like some punch-drunk hallucination coming on strong, he'll take a small sip
of air
and wonder what dark receding hallway his reality is skipping down now.
Come on, let's see what you got. The altimeter says baked and you got nothing but pulse.
A neon sign across the street buzzes on and off, a blinking beacon advertising cheap.
You wake up to find you're riding an empty on a train that doesn't even exist.
Should have taken first class, Pal. Full of feeble excuses
and half-hearted attempts, all you're doing is pissin' with the pups. No.

Naw, you ain't got a monkey on your back,
the poor son-of-a-bitch has got you on his . . .

Photograph by Christy Stiles

Rick Newby

Untitled

(after, and in memory of, Bill Stockton)

We drive the road through sere grasslands
and into watered canyons, seeking
THE NEW BRANCH OF THE PICASSO TREE.
We pass through this dusty town divorced
from modernity. We hope for a bracing vision.
Across the tumble-down bridge, dust
swirling behind, we encounter the spavined
gate, still upright but weary, and there they are:
FLOWERS AND DISTANT HOLLYHOCKS,
strident beyond the sagebrush, in this
LANDSCAPE IN OCHRE.
ONCE SOME POPPIES
splashed the slope above
the tangled garden and slouching barns.
Today magpies crack their jokes
from bare branches of THE DREAM TREE.
Even at the end, his hand faltering,
he painted his homely favorites—
CHINESE MOUNTAIN IN ORANGE
TWO WOMEN KNITTING
WEEDS ALONG THE ROAD.
Even at the end, his line unfailing,
he painted without stinting. And we are pierced:
By tenderness, by a quiet intensity
of yearning we can scarcely bear.
How came this BULL PINE IN BLACK
to speak of a MAN ALONE
who was never alone, accompanied
as always by his ELVIA,
her beautiful face—"when we are young,
we all are beautiful"—grave, radiant,
her limbs lovely as that FIG TREE IN TOULOUSE
where first she led him to taste undreamed-of
pleasures. Under that BLUE TREE–GREEN TREE
they danced at the center of a world unfolding
and delicious. Paris nights he dreamt of home:
the BOX ELDERS AT NIGHT, WINTER BRUSH,
and A SKIFF OF SNOW glowing under moonlight.
In dream he mourned, on hands and knees,
before the TOMB OF THE LAMB LOT TREE,
while coyotes wailed and waltzed
to their own music. From nearby hillsides

to distant coulees, the coyotes
mourn his passing, Six Birds in a Tree
chant condolence, the Sheep in Their Pasture
are bereaved beyond comforting. Even the Back
of a Chair, these straggling Brush Branches,
that Brick Wall, and those Two Potted Plants,
untended, yearn for his vigilant, irascible,
tender, imponderable, loving gaze.

Note: Text in capitals are titles of paintings and drawings by the late Bill Stockton of
Grass Range, one of Montana's finest pioneering modernist artists.

Night Vigil

in memoriam Fletcher Eugene Newby (1926–2002)

I find something soothing: dry crackle of leaves in wind,
                              darkened house,
                                    cold moonlight on crusted snow,
                                          dog and cat in luxuriant sleep.

After the darkness, void. After the silence, vacuum. Dust spirals soundless among chill stars.

He had us laughing: a tale of moose turds and savage appetites, tracks of an otter, scent of wild onion: a companionable walk, father with son, along the wild Stillwater in deepest autumn.

His totems: fur-bearing mammals—pine marten, fisher, fierce wolverine.

An enormous man reduced to ashes and paltry gravel. Relegated to a stout wooden box he will rupture at the seams.

"This is," he murmured, "a very impermanent life." Mighty legs splayed forlorn in the tiny bed.

I see him: a swaggering bull elk. With fine, intelligent eyes stained the blue of river ice.

In the half light at bedside, I matched the pulse of his breathing. Even as it slowed, even as the intervals stretched—breathless and peaceful—into distances.

"My beloved son," and he took my astonished hand, held it to the grizzled cheek.

Head tilted back, mouth ajar: rasp and rumble of the dying man.

He rumbled, unshaven, at parting: "I hope you've found me brave and swift—and seedy—as ever."

In last days, we shaved him. He sat, trusting and still, eyes shuttered against the light, razor scraping his slender cheeks, the broad chin, that tender, bloody lip.

He startled awake, to the snap and pop of a bending knee. Invented a sudden world of flame and double-hulled boats, of men with guns and ravening dogs. Is it flameproof, this world? he wondered.

He was grateful: "to have known love,
                         to have felt love,
                              to have loved."

Nothing more precious than that last glance of recognition.

A Day in the Life of a Tick

Here I am

just a tick

sitting on the tip

of this leaf

enjoying the day

tasting the air

balanced here

precariously

on the edge

of this cloudberry branch

by the side

of the happy trail

through the woods

sweet path of bliss

pine needles, etc.

Oh, look

here come some

humans

how I'd love

to fall off this leaf

get caught in some

long black tresses

yes I want

to bite your

neck but right now

I'll settle

for the back

of this leg

I believe I'm caught

in the threads

of this wooly sock

it's not exactly

what I wanted

but it will do

if I can only work my way over the edge of this sock and wedge myself down into the
soft and tender confines of this young girl's ankle won't it be heaven won't the blood go
to my head won't I be . . .

SLAP! Hey, honey, you had a tick on the top of your sock

it's ok I knocked it off

The tick sits stunned and amazed by the side of the trail
little stars surround his head in cartoon dizziness

A reporter steps up and thrusts a microphone into the maw of the tick and asks
How does this latest setback make you feel Mr. President?

My response to that is this: I will not be stopped!

Walking Helena with Nick

Saturday night, we walk downtown and all
is quiet, eleven o'clock, a few diehards
watching the stock car races behind their beers,
couple passing between dark buildings, waiter
out for a spit. No one hears or tries
to hear us. We feel secure in that, safe
in our own home town.

                         We encounter the works of man
in The Rialto, its empty booth out back.
No one eats up front but meals are prepared
in case someone emerges and veers to the counter
by chance from the neon saloon. The flat forehead
of the federal government silently broods at the end
of the mall like an Egyptian tomb, except
there are no statues or other humanity.
Lately abandoned for something more formally Roman
down in our new pseudo-Manhattan, it flakes, ·
the flat plastered walls brittle from sun and wind,
a crumbling ruin, aggressively regular
as every structure raised in Cold War brick.
Stones piled casually we observe
were not placed there by artists but workers in haste
to get the job done cheap and in poor taste.

We always walk our best when we walk free
through scenes of our own common history,
old hiding places we pass and note that now
the bushes are but sticks you'd stick out in.
You've grown almost as tall as a bass violin,
wavy-haired and driven to understand.
You see the problems with these buildings here.
Geometrically, there are no fractals
as in the trees, or for that matter, us
perambulating in the soft street lamps
with our expansive terms and calculus.

The pace of our true lives moves through our feet.
The view going by at such a speed we trust.
We speak with triangular references, sines,
cosines, in chemistry, free radicals
and dance through the lights that light up The Capitol,
skirting around it on our flexible bones
and timely interpretations. Saturday night,
we walk our town and The Universe in turn
together in peace, light years in our words.

from: **Letters from the Gospel Tract Society**
VIII. *Among the coal-dust*

I'm an old bird now, I've come for good.

If there's Death hid inside of it, there is, and let him come out.

> The spirit wandering, wandering
> wandering about the house.

In this house, my head,

slapping the baby,
that daughter of theology.

Early in the morning it revived my fury
to find that gentle heart

and I felt a hidden convict's
breathing in my spine,
a germ in the marrow.

I saw those animals,
their ironed legs:

that spectacle, disagreeable
and degraded.

> Remove the city,
replace it with poultice, baize,
rope-yarn and hearthstone.

Devote five minutes to the
rupture in my

mourning,

derived from sources
invisible and pungent.

Now I am but

a dry hard biscuit,
thrown sometimes into the slit
of your mouth.

Mother

Mother, I saw you
Hiding behind leaves and fronds,
Behind your steaming jungle hyacinth smells
Dripping their scent of secret
Violation.
You were so full of darkness,
A drunken, ragged bag of flesh
I married you twice,
Women whose breasts and hungry thighs
Touched like splinter wounds
Leaving me lost in their river smells
Seeming like love.

Mother, I breathed the swill
Of your poisonous breath
So full of shattered glass,
Violator of dreams,
Bequeathing me the death
Of your incestuous touch,
An emptiness
That steals all light,
A darkness that
Swallows life
Indifferent as the cunt of a whore.

I saw you fleshless
On the floor
A coughing, naked, paroxysm
Of death.

Thinking I might pick you up
One last time, I reached out,
But how do you hold
A devouring memory
That moves like ice
Through walls and dreams?

Mother, I kiss your sour mouth.
My frosty breath steams against
Your cold flesh
And rises against the sky
Light and pale
And far away
Like hope.

The Banquet

I sat in a crowded room away from you
at dinner and did not pray you'd come near:
did not imagine the hall our private room;
did not want to approach you with an air
of feigned indifference, leaving my meal-
time companions behind; did not conspire
alone to lure you into talk, to feel
the air crackling between us, the desire
like some doomed insect trapped behind the blinds,
pent up and buzzing, helpless; did not think
how easy it would be to change our minds
and reconcile, laughing over a drink,
our arms just touching; did not make a wish
for you—no, never dreamed a word of this.

Hunting the Immutable Delicate

In Florida a seventh grader
has shot his favorite teacher in the face.
"They were the best of friends,"
his mother tells reporters on the phone.
Red tissue lights the blackboard
like a pictograph.

Give us this day our daily bread.
Make me believe in something beyond myself.
Take me past the far hill
to the ridge where the winds terrify and sculpt
          the patient stone.
I had a child's heart once
that reached out and tore
into those who gentled themselves for me.
Hatred is not what turns hand against hand
but a kind of clinging fire,
a love gone to hunter
that tears something open
to carry away what's inside.

On a bench of hill a hunter watches
a river of caribou undulate across
the Arctic tundra's newborn flesh.
He kneels where some glacier has
coughed up a stone.
His spear points to a space in the air
where a caribou will step
carrying its heart forward in its chest.
The hunter makes his thoughts invisible to the
          gray-green hills
and breathes only thankfulness,
the quietest of exhalations.

Below him the tundra throws open
          a thousand throats to the sky.
The caribou dip in and out of ponds
doubling and halving themselves,
their antlers clicking.
Suddenly a space opens in the air,
a sable flank steps in.
Its dark heart asks a question
that the spear answers.
All bodies know one language,
the story of cup and bone,

of filling up and emptying,
of creeping forth, and being swallowed by the world.
Our lives are spent from breath to breath
pronouncing the unending name of God
until the hissing and the moaning are one,

as in that moment when a boy who loves
strides toward the face of one who loves him
and opens him like a book,
as in that moment when a caribou
folds into the tundra beside a yellow cinquefoil
and its last breath flies out across the grass.

The shape of that hunter's hand on caribou flank
is the shape of my hand at my throat,
or your hand on a newspaper
where you'll read of children hunting
the blood of what feeds them.

On Fellini's *Amarcord*

To war is human
To love
To err in the fog
and find a white bull
standing alone in the dark street.
Pantomime. Violin. Fascism.
The first Ferrari
Men dream fast
women
large bosomed and bottomed
young, willing to weather
inevitable seas, cigarettes and sparrows
Cold beauty, heels on ice
motorcycle desire
As death claims love
finally, for its own
realization arrives in an automobile
to the house where you grew up
While tortured souls execute credence
a march begins
Tall cemetery poplars stand
as they have always stood
intricate and blatant
against a toothless sky
Dirt under tires and feet
kicks dust into the
picture of a time
when one's death could be
more freely chosen
Nothing is real
Life is an act
milked from mothers' breasts
The unpleased bride is taken away
where, behind locked gates
politics, economics, science, religion, law
pound like heart beats
upon rattle-skinned drums
Firecrackers speak
in barber shops
Burning moving picture graffiti
Fart sounds made
in the armpit of tyranny
Black and white quiet
falls like rain
upon the woman
in a dress
walking the wind-waved beach
Plain-spoken truth
among bricks and soup.

Self Exile is a Strange Paradise

How many times (in a life) do we wash away the drift,
The drift of eyes, the drift of days?

We plant it and it dies.
Burn it, it rekindles.

The veil shatters and the image remaining disappoints us.
No face of gods, no shining angels,
No trumpets or sweetsmelling flowers.

Illusion removed, perhaps we know more
Than we know we know.
I am no Buddhist, but the perfection I seek,
The stilling of the waters,
An awareness of the completeness before me
Is not shattered, is not in need of mending.
Is whole and disparate at the same time.

But I forget that as I forget to walk with the creek
As it ices up. There are projects in town.
The sad excited meander into the city.
Out of the ice of my stare
My eyes quickly move away
Lest other eyes arrest mine,
Capture me in my confusion
And demand !
                    SPEECH

"How are you," they would ask.

And I would answer:

              "Did you see the color in the hills this afternoon?
              In the clouds? Did it remind you of anything, something
              you forgot long ago?
              Pawnee evening or Greek or an afternoon in
              Pittsburgh when the angel appeared to the Moravians
              and bade them rest?"

Outside town up a narrow hollow the air turns cold
As the approach of darkness settling among aspen
And sheperdia, pine and fir, subdues the wash of
Creek.

Twilight reflects lavender off the bare branches,
A stronger hue even as I look up from these lines.

*

Mouths of desire.
Riverine, silty, many colored
Swarms of sea life mouthing
The runofff of earth's sorrow
To feed again in turn
The caldron of nutrient air.

The true voice will shout through the false one.
The fool will go out and bring back the sun.
We will make a shining light in the darkness.

Poem in a Warm Winter

I will never be at war
with anyone that I will ever meet.
You might be at war with me
but I will never be at war with you
in any way at all.
Give me everything you've got
and I'll have seen it all before
or heard about it
in some dark and lonely place
where I might find myself
because you're at war with me.
But even in the deepest pit,
I will make a friend
of anyone I can.

from: Duende-Suffused Seferotic Incantation

Peruse my mind
And you will find
A Mirror
Striving to be
Dust-free.
Look into it
With Love
And what you see
Will so ravish you
That your Heart
Will melt,
And your Eyes
Will weep
Ecstatic
Tears.

* * *

My desire to be with you
Creates so much fire
That were I Orpheus returned from the dead
I would resume my long-silent lyre
And sing you a song of such longing
That the skylarks would swoon & the love-drunk,
Dervish-reeling stars in their spheres
Would weep copal & myrrh-fragrant tears
Of such consummate delight & pathos
That you'd swear you were hearing
The last swan singing its final chorus
At sundown, dreaming of dawnsongs past
And resurrections to come.

Cat Stretch

Slung low over gentle paws,
the hungry belly is so vulnerable.
I see my face, my sleepy eyes, in the water.
My whiskers bend the clear surface, my rough
tongue lifts the pure droplets. The sun
glows in the depths.

On the bending surface, there are other faces.
The most silly is the giraffe's. The silver
tongued devil browsing the treetops
enjoys every bone in its neck. The neck
arched over the water is so vulnerable.

The most frightening is the starving child's.
A swollen belly is overhung by a sunken face.
The dark eyes are so vulnerable, the small face
so old. I see the mother's breasts dry as paper
in the deep pool.

The ravenous belly is so vulnerable. So soft
and open, it swings beneath me. I am full
of trust and power. My breath expires
as I arch my back, till my lungs are empty.
Empty.

Outside the St. Ignatius Mission

We must be poets to hear from home
on nights like this. The moon
has a thousand echoes
in mud puddles all over town.

The old Mission looms behind
like something so terribly lost
that life anchors to the loss.
Its aged walls wane to ghost at night.

Through stained glass dim candles radiate
like the soul of something ancient
through the continuance of itself.
Home is a deeper place,

submerged here by the landing of this world
we cannot have.
God no longer thunders
from the sky, but whispers

in the ground. Home is where
children leave and where
the dead go. We stand
between, reluctantly chanting to ourselves,

stepping in time.
Are we the last? Going down
with no futures behind us,
our light merely decorative

and vision given up?
We go on praying to Earth,
and to us Earth says,
No.

Pelicans at Peoples Creek

(For my father)

This territory of my heart is known.
There are given mountains and deserts of it.
You have been relegated to the driest and loneliest parts.
This is something we both understand.
It is mutual.
No hard feelings.

So when driving north through a desolate prairie
on a cold spring morning
I suddenly encounter
right over the roadway
twenty huge birds, twenty white pelicans
wide gliding wings, black-tips,
swooping over a glimmer of frosty water
careening up over my car,
I slam on my brakes.

Standing on the graveled tarmac
mouth gaping, heart thudding . . .
What do they want?
Heart stopping birds flying low to the stubbled earth
forty miles from the Canadian border
lost from the Missouri.

They circle me.
In this pale light
it is you I want, to stand beside me
and explain as you did that first wet trout
awkwardly pulled to earth—
glimmering rainbows, gasping mouth
and you tell me how it happens
this life and death together.

So Daddy, I ask you again,
on this cold morning,
Why are they here
these water bound birds
hanging so close to the barren ground?
And why am I caught on this wide prairie
so far from any home I'll ever know?

The Drought Breaks

All day rain relaxes brittle grasses,
Softens bones,
Then clouds lift,
Follow the wind east—

Burst of sun before sundown,
I tread the moist ground,
Tension rivers off my skin—

Earth sighs
As I sigh
After making love.

An owl's voice opens.
Night breathes over my shoulder—

I take instructions from the night,
From my death, drinking in
The last red wine
Pouring over the world's rim.

Photo by Joy DeStephano

Sheryl Noethe

No Exchange of Livestock

It took me fifty years
            and countless attempts
to have normal sex. No booze, no sedatives, no chemical euphoria,
no alcoholic black-out.

No disassociating. No nearly dead drunk.
No "can't remember" or if I ever said no or stop.

No broken marriages. No betrayal. No danger.
No despair. No fixed silence. No blood. No infection.

No choking or gagging. No warnings. No threats.
No suffocation. No lying. No secrets. No night terrors.

No brothel. No money. No blood feud.
No exchange of livestock. No force.

No genital mutilation. No child brides. No angry God.
No gang rape.
No dusk to dawn curfew. No chattel. No vessel.

No choice.
No chance.

And where was God?
They say God saved the few children he could.
The rest, however, he kept.

Special Eds at Deaf School

"Have you cleaned your hearing aids?"
        "Did you sharpen your pencils?"
                "Stop laughing. Don't bother him."
                        "Ignore. Finish."

"Now," says the teacher, "I am going to write in your journals about myself,
        my family, what I like to do."
                Already the rabbit is at it, drumming his fingers at the back of his head.
                        The next step will be high-pitched cries, eye-lids pinking and fluttering.

Kyle is drawing elaborate, precise maps of every highway in the state of New York.

When I try to discuss the maps his teacher tells me not to encourage him.
                Venu is drawing hundreds of chocolate chip cookies in his journal, a gift for his
                        very stout teacher who hides boxes of them in her desk.

Venu has another bad report for his file.
                Indeed she talks. Her uncles, cousins, their babies, vacations, locations . . .
                        The boys draw a blank. Kyle is finishing his intricate map of Brooklyn.
                                "Okay," she says, "I'll make it easy for you. Just ask me one question."

The boys have forgotten about the journals. They are focused out the window, in case
                a plane passes, and when one does they shout and gesture, yelling "airplane!"
                        Kyle, master cartographer, with long bent fingers (they used to beat
                                deaf children's hands for using sign language instead of sitting on their

hands reading lips)
                thus appearing to be perfect around perfect strangers, has no question for her.
                        Face plum-color, she yells at the deaf boys. Close-up, her bulk a threat,
                                she shakes her fists. "Bad do!" she signs, "Bad do."

Frequently she lectures me about the need for appropriate behavior.
                Finally Kyle understands and begins writing in his journal.
                        The next morning his teacher asks to see his question. Eagerly, she reads it:
                                "Do you," he queries, "have to go to the bathroom?"

Splendor in the Grass

From sleep,
the bloodhound's tail
suddenly wags furiously,

racing
across fields. Galloping,
a laundry basket of ears and jowls aloft,
her suit a few sizes too big in the face.

Imagine:
an olfactory jungle, all shades of grey,
a billion scent ability.
Here, where a man walked days ago.

Maybe she is floating the Nile
with her snake-head attendants, slaves,
bowls of vipers and asps, urns of scented oil.

Now in the Montana midway sun
she sleeps on her blankets, and again
her dreams recall many royal positions.

One eye on the squirrels, one eye on her
white kitten, Queen of all she surveys,
kicking ancient dust into the modern atmosphere.

Donna

These colors are wrong. Too wet.
    Metal glints past this window and over the bridge.
Only the rage of light against nothing.

Now I am trying to avoid the falling places
    That I did not know were here until you
Went down one of them.

Your head shatters inside mine.
    I have no way to comprehend your violence.
These days since you are gone a drenched world

Jerks past too quickly.
    Everything tainted with your blood.
The car, the ground, my thoughts.

Now you are a spirit in the bush.
    No house to inhabit.
Only the mind can have you, re-forming the last minutes you left us.

Now certain trees are a delicate yellow-going-to-red
    like prized Japanese peaches wrapped in wax as they grow.

Messages painted in kanji stain their skin: health, long life, children.
    At the funeral your small daughters sang.

Little voices whispering about a bad dream and a gun
    I will never wake to this color day without seeing a pistol in your grip.

Stark faces, briefly muted by confusion, half-expecting your return.
    You will teach them what forever is. Hardly little girls now,

Proof that love is not enough. You are lost in an impulse too old,
    Too wicked to refuse. Every day I ride up that road with you, Donna.

And like the dead who return and have no voice, I beg you to wait.

2

Now you are queen and you are rain.
    No ears to hear the sorrow. A night of long dark.
Your youngest ran up to me, crying, Mama has run away and taken the gun.

Now your daughters will face the hard world of men without you.
    She cried in her sleep, said you came to her, rubbed her back.
Without hands. Under ground. Without hope. Over you bright Autumn
    Mourns.

All day long I forgot that you are dead.
    Until this afternoon, when a woman walked the edge of the road.
Dirt in my throat, brick and rust.

Deep Autumn. An impulse too old to resist.
    You had a dream and jumped out of it
By mistake.

How can death be more real? It has filled me with itself.

Now I see that I could not have stopped you.
    Last night was Halloween. We played at death with candy.
I lit candles in my window and along the path to my door.

You know who it is I was waiting for.
    Your ghost comes to my house and the dog shivers.
All wild-eyed and the world moves past us.

You are brooding in the truck, engine off.
    Clutching something in your handbag, knowing
This brief burst of energy and hope will not last.

A boy told me, years ago, that when he closed his eyes
    The world went black and fell away. He had no friends.
Who wants to be less than a shadow?

Your ghost is at the market, and in the low branches of the apricot tree.
    The dogs lies on his back, whines and shudders.
I cut a green apple into quarters, slide my plate across the table.

3

I danced with your daughters at my wedding.
    From the wet grass butterflies circled our heads.
I have photographs where you are laughing.

That afternoon, gone. You closed your eyes, we went away.
    Now we live in the afterlife. I see you in the pink cheeks of the living.
I wonder if they know they are haunted so.

Over a week since your funeral. You are beyond forgiveness.
   I cry from deep inside the locked trunk of my body.
I am trapped, you are free.

I desire my slavery to this quickening.
   Every molecule a feast. Love and fear, all of it.
Maybe I can live with you inside and we can share my life.

I will find something beautiful. I'll say, Donna, look.

Passion

Today my husband sandbagged Pattee Creek.
Spring run-off and all the rain caused floods.
When school let out he carried children
Across the rushing water.

When I was five our school flooded.
Firemen in yellow slickers
Carried us from the classroom.

When he tells me about his day
I am a child lifted over rising water
By a man she does not know
And set upon higher ground.

I embrace him, say, *Hero*
and he's embarrassed, his face colors.
I like this work, he tells me.
That's all he wants to say.

The minute I met him I remembered
How he helped me fly to dry land
A long time ago and I have been looking for him since.

Greyhound Villanelle

I watch the sun burn circles in the sky
and see the minutes vanish in the air.
The bus groans onward. Miles are spinning by.

I've swallowed moonlight sliced like ice cream pie
above the western mountains. I've been there.
I've watched the sun burn circles in the sky

and seen too many cities wane and die.
The highway passes through them, unaware.
The bus groans onward. Miles are spinning by.

I try to sleep, but only shut one eye.
The low, long drone of voices strums my ear.
All day, the sun burns circles in the sky.

In little towns, the families wave good-by.
The old men sit on benches; children stare.
The bus groans onward. Miles are spinning by.

I sit and feel so small, ask, "Who am I?"
The other voices murmur like a prayer.
I watch the sun burn circles in the sky.
The bus groans onward. Miles are spinning by.

Pick Up

What kind of finger to point? At which
map showing which right or southern turn? On
the newly poured shoulder, tar sucks at my shoe.

I'm willing to walk out here alone, gravel grinding
my heel, gray day and the surface of the road
one continual oatmeal. No one thumbs

a ride on the frontage road but me
so no one stops but you. Stories of fingers
in the psychopath's pocket, suspicion floats back

and forth in our first stumbling exchange.
You need me for company. I settle grateful.
Highway lengthens toward silence, hazard lights

reveal a wreck ahead: that bend and crush is
a pickup, passengers broken and bruised. The cop signs.
So we slow. I make up my third biography of the day

a circus carnie off hard drugs, catching up with my troupe
in Butte. Troikas for proof? Or tattooed star chamber,
miniature Space Needle, question mark inked

around my thumb. The bleeding undone beside you
helps me breathe. Eyes avert, driven waxy, in shock.
Could be you. Could be someone I love.

Every Decision

A cow elk lunges through dim
November morning, uphill across a road
and between black trees,

barely disturbing two feet of new snow.
You start tracking, rifle heavy
in gloved hands. Your partners

are miles away, circling to where
they don't know you will be. Each muffled step
blurs slower than heartbeats or cold

that reminds you how you are foreign,
vulnerable. Twenty years ago you rejected
the arguments of violence, swore

not to kill for anyone, even
your country, protested jungle deaths
more remote than democracy.

Now, after fifteen years of teaching
and poetry, you stalk an animal elusive
as the roots of doubt. Absolutes mean less

than how well something is done.
On a ridge above thick spruce
you see where she rested, her head

and one heavy ear outlined in snow.
Half a mile later she paused again
to browse tender willow,

then ran twenty yards. She may have heard
your delicate steps, smelled wool or man,
and chewed like cud an idea

that must keep moving or die. You wonder
how long you can listen, breath held,
and look for a dark back against

green and white. Is it more honest to kill
your own meat? You promise to waste
nothing, thank whatever God understands

how man and animal depend
on random death for meaning, a reason
to continue the repetition of step,

pause, step, pause until
you know that you can do it, can pull
the trigger, see her leap

suddenly sideways, run ten quick
yards, stand half-hidden, listening,
bleeding, until the second shot

drops her heaped brown and quiet.
All winter, this wildness
will feed you in your warm house.

You will remember cold hours,
hard curve of knife, steaming guts,
long pack out, and two echoing booms

that stab the quiet confidence
of every decision you make.

Crossing Montana

Everywhere in Montana
little white crosses
dotting two-lane highways.
Lilies, roses or
flaming leaf.
And who . . .
regardless of season kneels
at blind curves
and rock slides to do this?
Have you ever seen them?

Does gravel
remember the shape
of a body at high speed?
Do stones
retain the image of a young face?
Do hanging laurels
on metal crosses
stretch love, hollow-boned,
hollow-eyed, beyond
grief?

Love as a marker
of who died
on that three-cross curve,
that two-cross mile.
A plea to take it slow. A reminder
you no more hold
the face of life in your palms
than the thousand crosses
in Memorial Park hold
those flag-draped, beautiful
boys.

Winter

Sunlight this season for its own
sake. No thirst to slake, no need for shade.
No insidious heat or sensuous sweat
to sway the mind contemplating light.

Light slips past a cloud, slides down a wall,
infiltrates a window, illuminates
a painting by Chagall, slithers the hallway
under a doorway and up the other side.

Bursts into your room like near-death
experience, awakening the nearness
of the ever-present, omnipresent darkness.
Black tree in a snowfield casting no shadow,

brings one to mind, until the mind
sees only the shadow, dismisses
the tree as illusion. Light alone. Hell,
it is winter. Trees without leaves, light sans

heat. Shadows of the self. An old man
reflecting, back-lit by sunlight, shivers
remembering the future. May is not kind.
June rains don't always bring redemption.

Raindreams

Tent collapsed.
Greg's eyes wide:
Oh shit I'm sleeping in water.
Our light tries, but dies.
Pound stake with shoe!
(The ground resists--it's the Rocky Mountain Front.)

Nylon walls hold wind at a distance,
a boat carrying our sleepy heads
through familiar smells of old records,
hidden cigarettes, sweaty coins from the 50s when . . .
an invisible lizard climbs up my neck,
scurries through my hair to the base of my skull.

Kneads the skin yet doesn't break it.
Plants itself at rest on my head till
I feel the race of its heart in the muscles of my face.
I breathe heavy one two three four.
It's not leaving, wants to stay there,
but I can't take it,
shake my head to knock it off.
Expect claws to release, body to hit the tent.
He fades like the sound of a bell.
And I'm left with an ache, not sure if I lost
my friend or saved my brain.

Snowflakes

Snowflakes are fools God sweeps out of his kitchen.
Last night he emptied his dustbin all over western Montana
and we sure got a load of them
on top of everything else.
No wonder snow falls in such a light-headed mizzy,
makes us all silly,
immune, we believe, to all life's unreasonable demands—
our own children
when they become strange to us,
parents when they are frighteningly familiar because we've become
them, lovers
who want us to be their parents and children.

I spent this morning watching the border collie on Highway 200
chasing magpies from a road-killed deer. Entitled,
so spit-snapping-angry
that by noon when a golden eagle blew down
(that pitbull of raptors, known to airlift live lambs)
the dog hadn't yet had her first mouthful.

Had it been me I would have run home hurting for sympathy
and bit off my good husband's right ear,
kicked my own scat at my frightened children,
sung the family dirge: *Injustice!*
Then spent days as a field post, alone,
arm-wrestling with the winterly west wind.

At dusk the dog came home with one anvil-shaped hoof in her mouth,
    seemed glad to have it.

Back Again

We have lived a month
in a pit
in a rut
dug in the road.
The ladder
that lets me out
I'm ashamed of
though not enough.

Into Falluja

My father stands straight as the Joshua
rooted mid-corral. He catches loose reins,
swings himself across the naked
back of our palomino, heavy-
bellied and gnawing the dry hitch.
They cast a glance into a desert

drinking them in, sand soaking hooves, desert
barrels of water poking fetlocks. Like Joshua,
my father will try a soldier's distance of hitch
and stumble over cholla and sage. He reins
the horse from gallop to lope, a heavy
hand for patience. He knows the naked

risk of journeys toward water. Naked
faces of horse and rider wince in the desert
glare. Trees dot the stretch and each heavy
shadow is a person blooming alone—the Joshua
milky with frenzies of yucca moths, rains
of wings hissing at dark into the hitch

of yellow bulbs at limb's end. A hitch
in my stance makes a stranger shadow, like naked
bones, but really a child wondering if reins
take on life of their own, turn a father to desert
paths that leave him sleepy, Joshua
trees unmoved as his heavy

head makes a cradle in the sand. The heavy
river at the horizon moves in a crooked hitch.
I watch my father, the horse, each Joshua
they pass. The river draws them closer, naked
and clear in its offer to quench the desert
and the disbelief at a sudden smell of rain.

They're distant now and the jerk of reins
a guess. The horse's head droops heavy
as she dawdles over greaseweeds, desert
scraps not worthy of the blood it takes to hitch
the dry wisps from nearly naked
land, just shy now of the green turn—from Joshua

trees and snaky desert. I'll imagine the last hitch
of reins over riverbanks, heavy
with live oaks, beyond each Joshua, naked.

Photo by M. Stella McRoberts

M.L. Smoker

Grandfather Poem

His words are the ones no longer spoken, rising instead
from the steam in a kettle on the blackened wood stove.
He is almost blind but pours the cups with a steady hand:
"Coffee for this granddaughter, nighttime is on her mind."

Oyade wihamna. Hageji.
      Iyuha ezhedu wihamnabi.
           Oyade wihamna.

I pack fresh tobacco, begin the long walk.
Winds cut and cross over ravine, then plateau and ravine again.
I enter a door which faces south and do not feel ashamed
for entering this way. I think of a mother and father in sleep.
I know the distances we will devise,
navigate imperfectly.

Oyade wihamna. Hageji.
      Iyuha ezhedu wihamnabi.
           Oyade wihamna.

Mitugashi and I sweep down through the yielding riverbed,
walk the quiet rushes of the Mini Shoshe, then move north,
to higher ground. He motions toward the ponies as they rise up
and release their tears, large drops the size of ripe apples.
They dance then, as my mother and father shift in sleep,
dreaming to the rhythm of horses' hooves.

Oyade wihamna. Hageji.
      Iyuha ezhedu wihamnabi.
           Oyade wihamna.

Equilibrium

(In memory of Eric Levi BigLeggins)

1
After child after child after child, no one
believes in the cacophony of sirens anymore.

If only we could break back these bones
and form a new ceremony from each of our losses.

O mend our teeth from another dark stretch of road,
our rugged knuckles from another first of the month.

2
And still the children keep jumping from trains.
The people in town dream anxiously,
fire and iron licking at the corners of old,
handmade quilts. They have forgotten
the language of antelope and creek bed,
find in its place only one way to say
we are not responsible.

Today one man woke the callous offering
of a bird's beak and black wing
left on his doorstep at daybreak.
And what of all the other warnings,
of all the family lost because their hearts
were too heavy for them to carry?
If we could put these omens away, down in the basement
the door could be locked,
the mutter of crows left there to decay.

3
Next time and it will be the dance of chairs
and imaginary high speed chases.
It will require a fine sense of balance
and a song of stars.
Just the slightest slip of the rope
and the sky will be set
loose, the body
like a shift in the river's current.

4

The Bridge can hold, the Body can not, and our excuses
will do nothing to save us now.

We survive between these barbed wire
fabrications. We gather together in the middle of the night,
call out the names of lost cousins and friends who cannot
cross over to the other side because we keep
praying them back.
We ask so much of them: *slow the car down, don't jump,
don't let go, come back to us.*

But what are we really guilty of? – the blood memory of what
we can't forgive ourselves for.

5

Hollowed out grief becomes electric,
loosens a thousand storm patterns
in the marrow of ghost homes,
ghost children, ghost love.

Halving

(For Patricia Goedicke)

> "But later, among the stars
> what good is it–*they* are *better* as they are: unsayable."
> —Rilke

Rain on the just stripped deck – these things
often come upon us too quickly.
You had the presence of mind to bring in the chair's cushions
because I admit, I would not have made it in time.
If only I could find the presence, my own courage to ask:
did you regret finding one another after all that time?
Because I have also waited, taken my time more or less.
It has not been easy. It has rather been a sort of work.
And just now – sun on the deck, this large window pane,
a reflection of myself that reminds me of another:
who's body will we reach for in sleep,
long after it has gone?

You have decided, I have not.
When you talk of it, of all the moments between *here it finally is*
and *gone now,* I say why should we ever consider it
then marvel at the way your mouth still
tastes his name each time it rises from pink lips.
Just get on with it, I know you'd say
and I know you are right, about that and so many other
things. It just hasn't seemed clear, until now
when I know the angle of his jaw perfectly, can say just when
the color of his eyes might change. *See,* I hear you saying
out there somewhere, *I told you this is how it would be.*

Back Again

There are Indian women crying in the bathroom of Arlo's bar,
busted up, I guess – "you shouldn'ta messed with him again."
They're in there for so long we almost forget about them.
A trail of cigarette smoke edging its way along the crack near
the floor is the only reminder that they are still here, still with us.
Maybe it takes that closed-up-behind-a-locked-door feeling
to get them through another round. Mervyn asks the white guys
at the pool table if they want to play a game for their lives.
He grins and lets out his *Braveheart* cry so loud the whole bar
turns to see. He isn't afraid of much and maybe he knows that
playing for it all is the only way to go. He lands every shot
and one by one, they realize what a mistake they've made.
They wonder about that wager, edge their way up to the bar and
finally disappear out the front door. In the neon light of a Coors
sign Mervyn does his own victory dance around the pool table,
and maybe each step reminds him he is the one still standing.

Beautiful Existence

Death my friend is not long.
Wrapped in a tanned buffalo robe,
painfully I sank to the floor,
forcing my aching knee joints to bend.
I sat cross-legged.
Fumbling for my ceremonial pipe,
filling it with tobacco from a
small pouch; lit it.
Smoke wreathed around my head.
I felt for my drum and began a faint
Tapping on the taut rawhide.
The voice that once rang from mountain
tops, echoing along beaver streams.
Softly I sang a chant of death.
All is quiet.

Zu yea E Nanah

Zu yea E nanah
Woe yea be wache gra a
Ooshe ma ghee yea
Chay yea wa oo
Tay hon was che mnog knik

Ah bay do wajee
Cheek su yea
Zu yea E nanah
Woe yea be was che gra a
Ooshe ma ghe yea
Chay yea wa oo
Chanda ma seejaw

HayXada wake su yea
HayXada we cho nee yea
Wake su yea
O to weigh da a che yea
Wache mnage wache hay

Zu yea E nanah
Woe yea be wa gra a
Chay yea waoo
Wana tay hon wakinikt day no
EyaXa makocha
Zhe che yoda wa kinknt da
O yea ghee he unkash me yake su yeash.

You Went to War

You went to war.
Have pity.
I go crying.
I will not see you for a long time.

One of these days, I might forget you.
You went to war.
I will write to you.
Have pity on me.
I'm going crying.
My heart is sad.

I will not forget yesterday.
I will not forget yesterday.
When you come home to this place,
I want to see you again.

You went to war.
I'm going crying the long way home
To the mountain country.
That's the way I'm going home.
Do not forget me.

Magi cicada: Brood Emergence 1984

The year grandfather fell out of his skin,
I found a thorax, head, and flightless abdomen molted
under the winged seeds of the maple trunk,
an opaque presence standing-in for
something left, departed, went out—

transparence marking where eyes
had been eyes, where the molded
body and wings left
this cast of itself casting off
            the husk holding the shape
            of what emptied.

Here, touch this hollow space of
a body grown past its body,
cavity of what-was and air.

Sun pressing the pavement. Grandfather
gone. '84 and a thousand wet shiverings creep
through the trees. Forsythias, trimmed, occupy
their shapes while clematis scribble up the climb.

            Hold what's left
            of an emergence,
            a mass leaving—
                        this delicate ghost
                        emptied of the years
                                it took
                                to arrive.

. . . if it's on then it's on

ayo my spirit is rizing cause in faith theres healing.
showin unseen haters they can't break my meaning.
see i shake tha feeling, recreate my dream and
choose to play your game, if i play i'm keepin
any title that so many claim to possess.
arrows flyin in tha sky puttin tha game in distress.
warriors from tha past will remain in my chest.
you are my heros. guide my way in this quest.
i can see tha rain fallin and hear tha sky thunderin.
so it got me wondering why we stuck up in
this world of sin. my people sufferin, strugglin
just tryin to make it . . . stay strong thru tha tough times,
bullshit and tha hatred.
keep it true cause real eyes will realize the real lies they speak.
they could try to hold us down but we rizin to our feet.
we gotta over the obstacles that are placed before us
we warriors stay victorious . . . THEY CAN'T IGNORE US

October Suite

Old dog October arrives
half blind and wheezing,
limping its track
through ruts along the road.

I want to be worthy
of this waking dream:
my mother, before my birth,
kneads clouds at the counter.
Floured, rain-scent thick
as balm, they rise
in the far room and feed
no one. My father
walks the market, buys
hollow loaves, calls them
little worlds, little nothings.

First hike after the fires,
grasshoppers black
as burn. *Go on, hopper,*
fly away somewhere.
In the trees the scorched
knots look like people
clutching one another.

Tighten your purse strings,
my mother used to say,
your mouth is what you spend.
What if we learned to treat
each other as if a music
were barely playing?

To go to bed dusty
as unlit chandeliers,
and imagine it arriving
in a different season.
I used to think: December,
a windless day, bouncing
along the riverbottom until
an oak limb snags me,
swings under
a shelf of ice...But this
is the only time of year
and this the only cloud:
it sweeps the sky like a sheet
snapped from a clothesline.
We stand beneath
the burial of this light
lifting hands to whatever
we lift hands to. And like a tack,
the near-full moon pins
a black note to the ridge.

Robbed

Gerald was a quiet student in Native American Literature.
He wrote poetry and had a pregnant girlfriend. I did not
know his mother but know he grew hands and feet inside
her. On an unseasonably warm night in February while
heart-shaped lights stretched themselves across store
windows, a woman's son shot him in a moment. The
same night, my friend dreamed of a man with clean, white
hands who tried to strangle her, and she fought back with fists.
There's a war going on far away in the desert where women
speak with their eyes because the rest of their face is covered.
They wear gold shoes and the sons of other women are
killing their sons. A woman with empty arms stands beneath
the stars and screams to God because her son will never come back.

History of the West (two)

There is no key to sadness.
Rooms enter into one another
once you have found your way there.
I have decided for the sake of survival
that the pine needles are singing.
They are singing for someone
who has died. Singing in blue stitches
that belong on the hem of the tall woman's dress
as she crossed the plains, buzzards
and crows following her wagon train.
I have decided that mountains collect rain
the way memories are conglomerate.
It isn't just the notion of blood in the grass,
but that the notes falling through needles
can never be given back, or held as apology.

The Disinherited

Swerving across the genetically entrenched Indian Highway
Tribal houses sit quiet without windows
Ruling this place where truth has no audience
Community halls echo with bingo games and all-night wakes
Veiled bodies, like beggars, crawl on arrowhead roadsides
Joking that it cost a million dollars
Fluffed up promises made out of panic or allegiance
Dark secrets wield more license than the white doves you slaughtered
Leaving ancient bones and ash alone you take sleep too serious and
Pay too much attention to dreams and movements
Forsaking those closest to the hearts made small and innocent
Running a gauntlet of misplaced love

A Force They Could Not Control

The buildings are gone now.
Not a planned demolition, but
a matter of structures slowly
wasting away. Now, only the
brown and gray pictures remain,
left in boxes in the attics of
abandoned buildings and
in the minds of young children
now in bodies fully grown.

Set up by the war department,
a school for the children
of the beguiled and helpless,
taught to sew, to mend shoes,
to be carpenters or farmers,
and to touch secretly,
so that no one would know.
It was after all a school; and
they learned their lessons well.

The witnesses: places
quiet and cold; the kitchen, the pantry,
the dark, dank basement.
Tear stained faces, one by one.
One who closed his eyes real tight;
One whose face would turn blue;
One who lost his speech;
One fearful of running water.

The descendants sort through
old photographs; each face a memory.
This one became a rancher,
—rode the hell out of his horses.
This one killed himself,
—before his eighteenth birthday.
This one drank until he passed out.
And that one, that one,
passed on the legacy of touch.

They were told not to tell, but
they have, and look for their
lives in pictures and see
the cunning that taught them
touch and how to win the
trust of children. They did not
know that the touch would
lead them to the time when they too
would look upon the children with

a force they could not control.

Sunka Wakan Wacipedo

Otokaya kagapi,
Otokaya kagapi,
Otokaya kagapi,
Tehan amautan.

Šunka Wakan ahodawo,
Šunka Wakan ahodawo,
Šunka Wakan ahodawo,
Mini wicakuwo.

Šunka Wakan kuwanto,
Šunka Wakan kuwanto,
Šunka Wakan kuwanto.
Wayanka duzah han.

Šunka Wakan wacipedo,
Šunka Wakan wacipedo,
Šunka Wakan wacipedo
Eced waste wacipedo.

The Horses Are Dancing

The creation,
The creation,
The creation,
You looked at us.

Respect the horses,
Respect the horses,
Respect the horses,
Give them water.

"Horses, come over here,
Horses, come over here,
Horses, come over here."
See their swift running.

The horses are dancing,
The horses are dancing,
The horses are dancing,
And, they're dancing well.

from **Slip Face**

Early on she decided   already
there were enough words for things

Always she felt beckoned   Shuffled
each morning to the beet row   alder's
damp leaves & watched them settle bright
the river's floodplain   She could hum
some line pacific   walking the Kalama forty
        she did them by hand   With
a wheelhoe   Nine-thirty at night out
pushing it along thirty feet & stop   Turn
the wheelhoe over & hit it with a file
                                Then do it again
You can assert some things   Hang things
on others   Some people go on   In the shed
        she'd rack the wheelhoe   Other people
go on not knowing people ever

from Lake M

At night you craft your figurine

from stone,

    emperor
    gathering his maiden

into a porcelain gown

beneath a penetrant lamp

Her feet pristine, sharply white,
arched to quiet in the hall

Her fingers softly
on your arm

A bridge of birds
constrains her hair,
bowed above her faceless head

each finery crest displaying

Lean in to carve her mouth,
a tiny craze across her cheek

widening   *take me*

Before I am taken
by the light

I climb on the nightstand, singing

Photo by Kevin Martini-Fuller

Paul Zarzyski

The Day the War Began

I fed the dog and he was glad,
a bald eagle lit in the red
willows ignited
by a sinking winter sun, and prairie
chickens swept low in squadrons
over the hay meadow. Wind swirled
through glacial upthrust country, around
the nosecone rock named Haystack Butte,
old snow smoldering
during countdown. I breathed hard
toting haybales and grain
to the horses, to a field mouse
trapped in the slick tin feeder. Undaunted,
it sat on its haunches and lifted,
with deft fingers, a single
rolled kernel of corn
and ate in the warmth
inches from the filly's nostril. Three
lone coyotes on a trio of knolls
stopped me cold in the center
of a triangle of cry. They called to mind
the Hopi, their ancient tablet
warning of this war. East of here,
a crow-flown mile, the missile silo
lights, powered as always by the right
darkness, flickered on—less innocuous
in the dusk of that day. I forgot
I'd already fed the dog
licking his bowl clean a second time
within the war's first hour—so lovely,
the oblivion of another world
where instinct says, this simply, *live on*.

Wolf Tracks on the Welcome Mat

(For Hank Fischer)

But in the ruckus, in the whirl,
We were the wolves of all the world.
                    —Buck Ramsey

Long after dark, the big bad black
wolf, winded, knocks his softest
dewclawed knock on my straw door. He begs,
far too proud for handouts, a heart-
to-heart. Although a love poem is right
in the middle of whispering sweet
naughty nothings to me
as we stroll arm-in-arm
across the page, I ask him in,
fix him a thick ham steak and eggs,
Charles M. Russell's favorite.
                              The wolf
wants to pay me 7 million dollars for my trouble,
for the first home-cooked meal
he's eaten in eighty years,
but his pockets are empty
as a cowboy poet's pockets
the morning after drawing his pay
for Saturday night's show. Thus, the wolf
breaks into his rendition of *Moanin'*
At Midnight, a blues song so haunting,
so harmonious with the whole
toe-tapping cosmos keeping tempo,
it makes my guard hairs
bristle—silver needles tweaked
into each pore, the master
acupuncturist knowing exactly where
pain blazes its steepest trails.
                              The wolf circles
back to old Montana
as we go back to our childhood
homeground decades later to mourn
our own passing. We all crave, admit it,
what's vaguely familiar, the distant
glimpse of wild beginnings. We are all hungry.
We are happy. We all hurt and howl
louder the second time around
because we hope to learn to love our own
howling, as we love our healing—
all of us, from the same packed stage,
singing for our suppers.

Snapshot Gravity
(For Quinton Duval)

Sacramento. Outer city. Mid-autumn
Saturday morning. Mid-sidewalk. Pushed
in a wheelchair, the gray-stubbled man,
dapper in his red plaid
tam-o-shanter and matching lap robe,
comes grizzled face to grizzled muzzle
with a swaybacked gimpy Saint
Bernard-Rottweiler-maybe Lab cross
pushed on a limp leash. Traffic jammed,
frantic, we—two anxious friends
lamenting with country-western threnody
the body's plummeting descent—catch
between snatches of the oncoming
cars, the shutter-quick
glimpse of this soft
jowl-to-cheek encounter. The old
dog licks the elderly man's sad face
into hysterics, into a laughter
out of his past. Hands
invisible, arthritic, anchored in his lap,
the man turns the other cheek
for more, their fun-loving nuzzle
facing the busy street
as if posing for the impossible shot. Why not
lift this picture from the fixer
solution in our darkrooms
shingled with 8-by-10 action
glossies of good karma? Why not
paste the captionless snap,
solo and centered, upon the black
last page of the hefty album
gravity will likely someday keep us all
from lifting off the bottom shelf? Time
decides who becomes this earth's most
kindred—family, friends, acquaintances,
giving way to a blood-brotherhood
of strangers. Old man, old dog,
old portrait voyeurs—we all
take our over-exposed strolls
deeper into the residential flesh
where our hearts' silent horns rejoice
after each close call, every chance
collision of reckless love.

Feeding Horses In Richard Hugo's Fishing Parka

(For Ripley)

An easy swim-stroke every morning,
every evening, I float into the great
big man's coat, the thermometer
some days bottoming-out
at minus fifty, but still not cold enough
to cut the khaki canvas and wool
lined with quilted pink
satin that slides
lovingly—Dick might say—over feather
vest and sweaters. Bundled
almost to the tops of my moon boots—
half-bales grappled under each arm,
pockets filling with alfalfa leaf—
I plod like an astronaut or deep-sea diver
in a late-night Anthony Quinn movie
Dick likely drank to once
with glee. He liked his westerns horseless.
And goddamnit anyway, on those days
when wind swirls low
slipping its frigid giant-squid fingers up
suddenly under this coat
as if I've broken all the way
to my armpits through ice
of a glacial lake we fished
until our Olys froze
mid-sip, us cursing in cracked Italian
our luckless quest for the fur-bearing trout—
on those days, I'm with Hugo
howling…*and to hell with horses, too*!

The Hand

(For Alan Thompson)

In South Africa, a white aristocrat grabs
the hand of an elderly black man
sitting in the dirt on the edge
of a lush crop. The white man
picks the black man's hand up
as if it were a self-serve gasoline nozzle,
pulls it toward a reporter
and mechanically squeezes the wrist
to spread wide the thick callused fingers
and palm. The white man holds his own hand
open side-by-side. *Do you see
the difference?* he asks. *What
does his hand look like to you? How
can you say we are the same?*

Do you see the difference? he asks again,
the reporter stunned by what he is hearing,
while the black man sits inanimate,
his working cowboy hand
filling the camera's close-up lens
with a landscape of canyons,
coulees and arroyos, buttes and mesas, mountains
and plains the black man might have ridden,
hands shaped by pistol grip, lariat, and reins,
had he been born of another geography
and time—just another wind-burned hand
of a *cavvy* man, sinew and knuckle,
flesh and blood, pocked, porous, scarred,
and dark as lathered latigo. The hand
alongside the aristocrat's
tissue-paper appendage always reaching to take
even another man's hand, and own it,
and hold it open, because he knows the fist
is as big as a man's heart
and *this* is the difference he fears.

For the Stories

Deep blue backdropping the bucolic autumn
embroidery of sumac, maples, spruce
bordering dewy hay meadow sparkling beneath
the sun rising giddier than usual that day
with anticipation, Charlie Parker
steps from his smoky touring car
into the peculiar air of a rural morning,
builds his horn and blows
choruses for a lone cow
because Bird heard animals love
music, too. I picture it this way:
the intimacy of each frosty note
scaling a five-wire fence
between Bird and Holstein—she had to be
because I can hear Parker telling later
how he blew for *a black cow*
with a little white on it,
maybe for the same reason he played
Hank Williams on the juke,
not for love of rudimentary chords
but *for the stories, just listen*
to the stories, man, he'd tell
his fellow cats razzing him
about his white-blues taste
in tunes. It's pure hearsay
that the puzzled cow—though chewing
her cud in tempo with Bird's
swaying saxophone
shimmering in the low sun, his fingers
slowly crawling over the keys—
was not impressed. I don't buy a word
of it. Rather, I picture a bedraggled farmer
thrilled out of his drudgery
the night Betsy's milk output tripled for life
after an otherwise run-of-the-mill day
when our world moved four bars,
four measures from its normal
orbit, stirring, in turn, the whole
infinite universe toward
the unpredictability of what is
musically possible, humanly perfect.

For One Micro-Chronon of Time

Not the collisions and mirror image story
caving-in-upon-story-
collapsings of all hope,
but rather *this* footage is what
we must run and rerun
to believe we can live on. Notice—this time,
your eyes closed, your heartbeat
stilled—how those there witnessing
the one-by-one acceleration of the tower's top floors
buckling, all threw their arms up
in New York unison. Against the looming black
weight, imagine, feel, how they strained
to lock into place with their power-
lifting lumbar—with their knees,
shoulders, elbows, fingers, toes,
sinew and soul—the tonnage
they knew they could hold aloft
like the song's superhuman coal miner hero,
Big Bad John, hoisting a timber
while trapped men *scrambled*
from their would-be graves. Mere geologic
disaster of earth and rock,
it's true, is a far far cry
from thick concrete, steel girder, plate glass
falling from love and hate
forces locking horns so high above
not even the most faithful incarnate should hope
to hold back the heavy downpour of hearts
stopping cold. But they did. Watch closely
this time-lapse frame-
by-frame replay
pulsing so, so slow, and you, too, will
believe how they held, for the most truthful
infinitesimal moment, the whole
world's molecular make-up
of evil at bay—how they held, and they held.

Making Peace

Start with apples. Pick as the frost lifts
in a nimbus of crows and the orchard rings
with harsh predictions. Pick a dawn
when the children of three nations
are pulled slack from the same rubble,
when a crowd of gaunt Somalis tease
a pile of dead white men
and tanks thunder
in Russia. Pick
indiscriminately.
Take pale fruit from the shelter
of inside limbs, any warped, wasp-gutted
end of season red left hanging. Pick fast
from a bad perch in an old tree in the chill
of early winter warnings. Pick them all.

Call in sick. In Detroit, two boys are shot
in a game of Truth or Dare and a man of God
admits the rape of parish children. Wash the apples
thoroughly. Use the sharpest knife, open them
with slick snaps, pile them to the lip
of a four gallon stock pot, add a dash
of pure water and cover to hurry the fire.
Boil until the juice gutters and pieces
bleed together, until the bulk of it sinks
in the stroke of a wooden spoon.
Save the flesh in a clean pot. Bury the rest
trowel-deep beneath the asters. Water well.

Throw open the kitchen windows. In Butte
a girl gives birth in a toilet and flushes
and flushes. Taste the sauce, determine
a ration of sugar, measure spice
in a cupped palm, cloves by the pinch,
vanilla by drops. Jack up the fire
until the kettle ticks and the sauce rolls
with sores that burst and heal in clouds
of steam. Seal it all. Make tea.
Sit where the late autumn sun will touch
the flawless lines of fifteen Mason jars,
capped and hot to the touch. Listen
for the kiss, the quiet straining
of lids drawn to the brink, quivering
until the first gives in and the others follow
like bells.

A passage from the story, **Bones of Joseph**—

The double doors were thrown wide and music welled into the dark
lot where already young couples melted like deer into the verge of cottonwoods
and beneath the light above the door miller moths swirled and clattered thinly
on the metal dome. Older couples moved about the sanded floor
as compatible as draft teams and even the heaviest of them seemed
as weightless as the fluttering millers, turning the years to bald falsehoods as in
their boots they floated incumbrous as sprites. When the music
stopped they stood looking at each other in a kind of wonderment
to find themselves so fettered with age when it was not three or ten
or twenty summers ago they'd slipped with a blanket
under the whispering canopy of cottonwood leaves.

Anastasia's Afternoon

She raises the screen door latch
with the back of her hand, her face
to the steady run of the creek.
Her feet know the step to stir
the dog from, the step to sit on
and where to set the bag of plums,
the paring knife, the scoured pan.
She waits for the house to die down
behind her, cool air to lift
her shirt, ease the slope of her back,
the knot in her head,
into the downstream run.

Time to travel the syllables
of her name—the charge of the ranch woman
who could have murmured Shirley Mae
or Jane but named her newborn
Anastasia, intending perhaps
a wistful hint of Athens
for mule deer browsing the buck brush
along Nevada Creek. Or hope for
resurrection among the onion rows.

The knife blade warms the worn step,
plums stain the brown paper purple
in August heat. Anastasia's fingers
work out the pits, her thoughts work back
across the hay meadow to circle the child
curled between her hip bones. The creek runs
down the mountain alone. After the plums,
new potatoes to dig, after the spade thrown
aside, a bath, fresh clothes
and kitchen words to exchange for news
of hay, of horses, of water level.
Anastasia rises, licks the juice
from her fingers, thinking of yesterday
when her men rode in.

The Silver Grill Café

A dark girl with straight black hair
tends bar in Alberton. Today she stares
at her hands on the formica counter.
The light is dull in this café
this morning in winter. She looks
at her fingers, the formica, she tries to mend
the broken glass and bourbon in her head.

She does not want to order anything.
No coffee, no breakfast. She wants to forget
the people she served all night in the bar.
The solitary woman who would not talk,
the cruel man and his wife, the drunk
who mumbled to the bar. No, she will not
remember them or their demands.

The beautiful dark girl in Alberton
rises and turns to the window. She sees
that the low clouds have a color like pearl.
She orders a burger. Brief sun gilds
the painted letters on the glass and dark
cliffs glow. She will take it home and watch
the trains pull out along the river.

Outside, an old woman walks toward
the Silver Grill. She lives alone and fears
winter, fears ice and falling and broken
bones. It took all morning just to get this far.
The girl inside can tell that woman once
was strong and quick and scorned the cold. She opens
the door, helps her up the icy steps.

The long dark girl can hear the street, the loud
voices of railroad men eating lunch
in this café. The old woman has coffee.
The girl takes her meal and walks out
into snow, and with each step knows we are all
beautiful and deadly in our time.

Driving Montana

The day is a woman who loves you. Open.
Deer drink close to the road and magpies
spray from your car. Miles from any town
your radio comes in strong, unlikely
Mozart from Belgrade, rock and roll
from Butte. Whatever the next number,
you want to hear it. Never has your Buick
found this forward a gear. Even
the tuna salad in Reedpoint is good.

Towns arrive ahead of imagined schedule.
Absorakee at one. Or arrive so late—
Silesia at nine—you recreate the day.
Where did you stop along the road
and have fun? Was there a runaway horse?
Did you park at that house, the one
alone in a void of grain, white with green
trim and red fence, where you know you lived
once? You remembered the ringing creek,
the soft brown forms of far off bison.
You must have stayed hours, then drove on.
In the motel you know you'd never seen it before.

Tomorrow will open again, the sky wide
as the mouth of a wild girl, friable
clouds you lose yourself to. You are lost
in miles of land without people, without
one fear of being found, in the dash
of rabbits, soar of antelope, swirl
merge and clatter of streams.

Old Folks At Jaker's Restaurant

The pale old woman leans to one side.
Her head disappears under the table.
Something rattles like pebbles on tin.
Her daughter, also an old woman,
apologizes to the waiter.
"She's just out of the hospital.
Her heart is weak as paper."

"I got a little dizzy," the woman says,
reappearing. "I'm not hungry any more."
She pulls herself upright in the booth,
smiling shyly. She stands up in the aisle
between our tables, strong as straw, her
farm-wife knuckles, white arthritic stones.
"I died twice in the hospital, sir."

"She's dying again," I tell my wife.
I stand in time to catch her in my arms.
I'm not strong enough to do what
would have been easy twenty years ago
but my watchdog, *Pride*, won't let me beg off.
I pick her up, carry her to my car,
my heart beginning to stumble. I cough.

Her eyes, banked with fog
but sharp with humor, measure me.
"You're too goddamn old
to be doing this, kid," she says.

Stones

If stones were silver
like my grandmother's spoons
that came boxed
and wrapped in black
two weeks after she died,

I'd cherish them, too,
dip oatmeal, fresh sliced peaches
floating in thick cream,
stir fragrance
of wild, raspberry tea

and sift cinnamon
onto egg custard—spice
that will float, crisp
when three hundred and fifty
degrees has done its job.

And I'd shine them each Friday
like she did the spoons
and lay them, glowing,
side by side on crocheted mats
I'd hook like hers—

If stones were silver.

Riders' Block

Tonight they're trying, once again,
With pencils poised, impatient pen,
To scribe the ultimate in verse.
They write, erase; they chafe and curse
In roundup camp, in barroom smoke
To braid in rhyme the latest joke.
The quest to fill the current rage
For cowboy pomes, to mount the stage
In Elko, is their hearts' desire.
They writhe in rage beside the fire.
Each stanza's formed, in diagram,
In foreheads throbbing with iamb.
Prepared to drop each "G" in "ing."
Slick metaphors are poised to spring.
All they need's a topic, yet
Each mind is numb. They squirm and sweat.
They quick-draw blanks. They should be fannin'
Bull's-eyes aimed at Elder Cannon! *
Why! They could rival Badger Clark!
If mental coils produced one spark
To light this black hole, filled with doubt.
But no! No mark, they missed him out.
To hell with humor! Nostalgia then?
A saga of bold saddlemen?
A cutting swipe at dudes? Or women?
Or bureaucrats? Their minds are swimmin'.
Damn Zarzyski, Michael Logan,
Who never lack a theme or slogan
Or inspiration for a rhyme.
What's their gimmick? Why's it I'm
Stuck here rimrocked, thinking zero,
When I could be a western hero
On Western Horseman's poet's page?
A sagebrush rhyming cowboy sage.
My powder's wet. The well is dry.
Calliope has passed me by.
Take heart, all you rhyming pards,
The West is filled with want-to bards
Just two quarts low of inspiration,
Filled tonight with great frustration.
Horse rider's block, you're right, 's a curse,
But pardner, there's one problem worse:
It's them that's got but zilch to say
But goes and writes 'em anyway.

*First director of the Cowboy Poetry Gathering in Elko, Nevada

The Fool and The Knight

Hold and sheath thy blade,
       I bring but merriment.
Whilst thow, a slave of war,
       From deaths own stronghold sent,
Would with thy wand of steel
       Clame by might the way
And turn from white to red
       This snow on Christmas day.

I own thy greatness, noble Sir,
       A fool I am, thou seth
But who is welcomed most by man
       Merriment or Death
If merriment be ignorance
       And war is wisdoms school
With gory blades as teachers,
       I am, thank the Saints, a Fool.

Biographical Notes:

Sandra Alcosser's most recent book of poems, *Except by Nature,* selected by Eamon Grennan for the National Poetry Series, received the Academy of American Poets' James Laughlin Award. Alcosser has received two National Endowment for the Arts Fellowships, and her poems have appeared in *The New York Times, The New Yorker, The Paris Review, Poetry,* and the *Pushcart Prize Anthology.* She founded and directs the Master of Fine Arts Program in Creative Writing at San Diego State University as well as SDSU's International Writers Summer Program at National University of Ireland, Galway. She is Montana's first poet laureate and the 2006 recipient of the Merriam Award for Distinguished Contribution to Montana Literature.

Minerva Allen, the daughter of an Assiniboine-Gros Ventre mother and a French Chippewa father, grew up on the Fort Belknap Reservation with her grandparents. She is a life-long educator. She entered school at age five speaking Assiniboine and Gros Ventre and learned English so quickly she served as tutor for other students in her elementary school. Minerva holds a bachelor's degree in education from Central Michigan University, a master's degree from Montana State University–Northern (Havre). She has worked as Head Start Director at Fort Belknap, Bilingual Director and Federal Programs Director at the Hays–Lodge Pole School District, and served as President of the Montana Bilingual Education Association. She is currently "retired" but continues to actively be involved in varied activities, including writing, serving on boards, working with senior citizens, generously giving of her time as a language and culture resource person. She is the mother of eight children (and raised six more) and enjoys numerous grandchildren.

Alex Alviar lives in Missoula where he is ungainfully exploited as an adjunct professor by almost every post-secondary education establishment within an hour drive of his home. When not busy being underpaid, Alex reads and skateboards more than he writes. He also writes freelance for local magazines and teaches poetry in various public schools via the Missoula Writing Collaborative. Currently, he's considering ditching the teaching gig for an electrician gig or something with benefits. Update: Alex has just joined the Liberal Arts Department at Salish-Kootenai College as full time faculty. For now, his electrical dreams will have to wait.

Hannah Bissell writes: "I wrote my first poems when I was eight years old, just after the last snow disappeared from our yard. They were about the way the world felt when the sun came up and winter melted away. Words are the best gift we are given. At times I get blocked, and my mind gets cobwebbed. But the cobwebs melt away, like the snows melt away, and I'm free to write again." When she's not writing a new poem, Hannah hunts and fishes with her dad. She's a sophomore at Flathead Valley Community College and plans to transfer to Washington State University-Pullman.

Judy Blunt compares the thirty years she spent on a Montana cattle ranch to "the unholy union of John Wayne and Gloria Steinem." It just couldn't last. She's the author of a bestselling memoir, *Breaking Clean*, and the recipient of several nonfiction awards, including a PEN/Jerard Fund Award, a Whiting Writers' Award, and a National Endowment for the Arts Fellowship. In 2006 she received a Guggenheim Fellowship to write essays about Montana ranch life. Judy teaches creative nonfiction at the University of Montana-Missoula.

Zan Bockes earned her MFA in creative writing from the University of Montana and claims to be a direct descendant of Bacchus, the Roman god of wine and revelry. Currently she is prospering as a Residential Sanitation Specialist for her own cleaning service, "Maid in Montana." Zan has been published widely in numerous magazines and has been nominated three times for a Pushcart Prize.

Bill Borneman lives in Helena, Montana, with his wife, Patti. He works as a contract painter, dabbles in the "book business" (www.bedrockbooks.com), and plays Lo Prinzi guitars. His degree in philosophy from The University of Montana aids him in each of these endeavors. Borneman is currently a member of the poetry performance quartet, The States of Matter, a group devoted to the sonic realization of poetic occurrences. He is perhaps best known as the genial host of the literature reading series, "Naked Words," held in the Rathskellar of the Montana Club in Helena.

Pansy Bradshaw is a noted writer of both travel and erotica, and ("most humbly," he says)...a poet. He moved to Beaverhead County in 1996 where he lives in a trailer, works as a nanny and walks, literally, in the footsteps of Sakagawea. He does a great deal of public speaking on a variety of subjects from "western scriptures to queer kulture."

Cedar Brant is a field biologist who spends her time identifying plants, counting elk, and taking note of growing patches of weeds. Cedar does fieldwork as a way to witness the Montana landscape and to take stock of what Montanans could lose to the steady influx of weeds and development. She grew up in the dandelions and snowberry bushes of the Flathead Valley, home-schooled with three other families. The home-schoolers formed a club, Children for Wildlife, and traveled along the Canadian border, radio tracking a wolf pack during the years of heated conflict over the Wilderness Bill and wolf reintroduction. She makes her home now near the confluence of the Bitterroot and Clarkfork Rivers.

Frederick Bridger lived three separate lives in various parts of the world before becoming Instructor of Literature and Creative Writing at Montana State University-Great Falls. He began writing and publishing again only recently after a 25 year hiatus. He feels sufficiently removed and safe from past events to synthesize them into poems that he composes in his head westbound in his truck, or at his isolated cabin on Rogers Pass, where, he says, "I can stand naked at the screen door or piss off the porch and it doesn't matter."

Carole Bubash is from Anaconda, Montana, granddaughter of Croatian and Cornish immigrants. An early poem—about the seasons—was "published" when a seventh-grade teacher tacked it on the class bulletin board. Much later her first published short story appeared in *TriQuarterly*. Carole studied writing with Jack Barsness at Montana State University and with Richard Hugo at the University of Montana. She taught bilingual creative writing at the University of Texas-El Paso, and now landscapes with plants and rocks.

B.J. Buckley writes: "A Wyoming girl born and bred, I ended up in Montana after a friend persuaded me to answer one of the ads in the St. Ignatius, Montana, *Cowboy Sweetheart Newsletter*. The gentleman in question was a blacksmith and machinist, and there was no livestock involved. After a brief correspondence and one extremely congenial meeting, I pulled up stakes, and moved to the 8x16-foot cabin in the woods near Florence, Montana, where we still live, without running water or electricity, in the company of three dogs and a cat."

Philip Burgess was born and raised on a small ranch near Sidney, Montana. He is a Vietnam War Veteran. He earned a counseling degree from The University of Montana and worked for many years as an advocate and therapist/counselor for veterans in Missoula. At present, he spends his time "daydreaming and traveling around the back-roads of Montana."

Heather Cahoon was born and raised on the Flathead Indian Reservation where she is an enrolled tribal member. She earned an MFA in poetry from the Creative Writing Program at the University of Montana and recently also completed an Interdisciplinary PhD in History, Anthropology and Native American Studies. She has taught at the University of Montana and Salish Kootenai College.

Dennie Carpenter writes: "For most of my life, I was the victim of my own ignorance. I was full of hatred and prejudice; anyone who was not like me, I believed, had no place in this world. I quit school at age twelve, and I did farm work. When I turned eighteen, I enlisted. Trained as an Armor Crewman, I learned to kill without prejudice. The tanks I trained in are now in a museum or on the lawns of some town square." Carpenter lives in Bozeman with his wife and four children. He is a student at Montana State University.

Dave Caserio writes: "As a kid growing up on the south side of Chicago, I badgered my father, a steel worker in the mills—"Why can't we move to Montana?" But we never did move. In my eight-year-old mind the west was all clear running waters, bears and otters, mountains and snow, wind and tall grass. Perhaps this innocent, pristine illusion was fostered by my Italian grandfather who claimed to have been born in Butte while his actual birthplace was Lansing, Michigan." Dave is the recipient of a Fellowship in Poetry from the New York State Foundation of the Arts. He currently lives in Billings.

Ed Chaberek claims he hasn't roamed outside the Montana state line since 1987. He writes: "My journey to Montana started when I co-authored the 'Red, White, and Blue Pickle Hoax.' My pal and I figured what with the 4th of July coming and America mired as usual in a mess, why not a 'pickle' expressive of the pickle we were in (and are). Lo, suddenly in our imaginations was born the patriotic horticulturalist, Abel Grus, and his fabled brining process which produced 'patriotic pickles.' All went well until the story hit the national news and reporters everywhere were searching to interview the fabled Abel Grus. The road to Montana seemed easy-going after that." Ed lives in Superior, Montana.

Casey Charles came to Missoula in 1993 to teach English at the university. He started writing poetry after meeting his partner, a painter from Whitefish. While teaching Shakespeare at the University of Guanajuato, Mexico in 2001-2002, he published his first poem in Spanish and became associated with the San Miguel Poetry Week, where he has returned to study. He dedicated his first chapbook, *Controlled Burn* (Pudding House Press), to his mentor and colleague Patricia Goedicke, who died in 2006.

April Charlo is the proud daughter of Jan and Victor Charlo. April is a member of the Confederated Salish and Kootenai tribes. She has made Salish an important part of her life when, at a young age, she realized that the language could be lost. April's passion for the revitalization of the Salish language has led her to join forces with the Native American Language Teacher Training Institute. She plans on becoming a fluent speaker and a teacher using her speaking abilities for the betterment of her people.

Victor Charlo writes: "I was a stutterer, 'Wheeeeere is my coat?' I would say. They sent me home from first-grade because of it. I had my new clothes on and all. And they teased me, too. My father said, 'Boy, you're really smart. You finished school in one day.'" Vic is the great-great grandson of Chief Victor Charlo of the Bitterroot Salish. Through lineage, he is recognized as a spiritual leader.

Phil Cohea studied under Richard Hugo at The University of Montana from 1972–1974. He moved to Helena in 1975 where he co-founded with Rick Newby and Lowell Uda a literary magazine, *Scratchgravel Hills*. After publishing a handful of poems, Phil entered into a hiatus of twenty years during which he raised two sons and produced an album of songs, *Lone Western Stranger*. In 1996 he returned to writing poetry at the age of forty-eight and is assembling his first book of poems, *Last Drink with Sir Walter Raleigh*. Phil has also recently recorded another song collection and is working on a young adult novel.

Aunda Cole was born in 1913 in Ohio. Her daughter writes: "My mother could have been a concert pianist but chose to marry Eugene Cole, a barnstorming pilot. After WWII the couple and their daughter, Diana, moved to Kalispell, Montana. My mother loved the music of the mountains, flowers, meadows, lakes, streams, and birds. She brought her piano skills to poetry, recording her adventures in Glacier National Park." Aunda died in June of 2000.

Alison Colgan grew up in Poplar, Montana on the Fort Peck Indian Reservation. She is an enrolled member of the Sioux/Assiniboine tribes. After attending Poplar High School, Alison relocated to Billings to attend Montana State University-Billings where she earned a Bachelor's degree in English. She has been a senior editor of *The Rook*, MSU-Billings literary magazine, and she has served as a volunteer for the High Plains Book Fest and the Montana Poetry Project.

Corrina Collins was born in New York City. She moved with her family to Montana during grade school and, even after extensive travel, she doesn't stay away for long. Corrina is a graduate of Bennington College, where she studied literature, writing, and philosophy. Now living in the hills west of Helena with her son Eamon, Corrina plans to live and work in Denmark, Japan, Brooklyn, and Portugal before settling for good in Montana.

Dorrance ComesLast, aka **Native Siouxperman**, is a member of the Dakota Sioux nation from the Fort Peck Reservation. Born and raised in the traditional ways of his grandparents, Clifford and Vida Youngbear, Dorrance has spent all of his 22 years in Poplar, Montana. About his life and work, Dorrance says, " I'm still followin tha wayz of our ancestors…and alwayz puttin TUNKASIDA (GREAT CREATOR) first before anything else…try to stay positive and help my people that are struggling…i'm drug and alcohol free…have been all my life and intend to stay that way…" Dorrance is an up and coming Native rap artist who has already produced several albums on his independent label, Still True Productionz. "I'm rappin for my native nationz across tha globe…we gon rize together."

David Dale, a native of Helena, Montana, was a public school teacher for many years, now retired. He received the MFA in creative writing from the University of Montana-Missoula. He has published five collections of poetry, all with Big Mountain Publishing. He and his wife of 46 years make their home in Big Arm, Montana.

Donna Davis is a poet, actor, attorney, and a sometime philosophy and humanities professor. She is a Tumblewords (a WESTAF program) teaching poet and one of the original Poets on the Prairie for Writer's Voice, a national program to bring writing and writers to communities all across the country. In her enthusiastic way, Donna has brought poetry to thousands of students ages 8 to 80 in a wide variety of settings. She is also the Poet Laureate of "Waste Not, Want Not," a monthly feature of Yellowstone Public Radio.

Madeline DeFrees, like Socrates in ancient times, belongs to a peripatetic school. She walks nearly every day—sometimes as far as five or six miles, honing recalcitrant lines of her poems as she goes. "Pendant Watch" is the first poem she wrote after moving to Montana in 1967. She was 48 at the time and is now 87. She lives and writes in Seattle.

Rick DeMarinis confesses he "started off as a poet but didn't make the cut." Since then he's turned to "less punishing forms," short stories and novels. He's published six collections of stories and eight novels. Rick taught creative writing at a number of institutions, the University of Montana among them. He is now retired and lives with his wife, Carole, in Missoula.

Michael Devine, with his *Mainstreet Show* in Livingston, has offered audiences an eclectic mix of music, drama, poetry, political satire and storytelling. Devine draws inspiration from the quirks and peculiarities of his fellow Montanans whom he describes as "a wealth of contradictions."

Chris Dombrowski was born and raised in Michigan and educated at Hope College and in the MFA program at the University of Montana, where his honors included a Poetry Fellowship, a Matthew Hansen Endowment grant, and the AWP Intro Award. He has worked as a cabin painter, freelance writer, river guide, poet-in-the-schools, adjunct professor at UM, and for a Missoula homeless shelter. His poetry has appeared nationwide in journals such as *Bloomsbury Review*, *Colorado Review*, and *Crazyhorse*. He lives with his family in Missoula.

Roger Dunsmore writes: "It must have been in my early 20s that I read the first modern poem I understood, that touched me—'I sing of Olaf glad and big' by e.e. cummings. Lines like, 'I will not kiss your f.ing flag,' and 'there is some s. I will not eat,' and the overall narrative of a heroic conscientious objector who is beaten and thrown into a dungeon, moved and aroused me. I remember thinking, 'Why, they really are saying something, some of these poets, and, by god, they're going to tell the truth.' That one poem opened a door for me, let me see that poems could mean things, things that mattered, and be understood by mere mortals like myself." Author of many books of poetry and a collection of essays, *Earth's Mind*, Roger Dunsmore teaches at the University of Montana-Western (Dillon). A gifted and generous instructor, he is much loved and admired by his students, colleagues, and community.

Tom Elliott retired from his position as managing partner of the N-Bar Ranch near Grass Range. He's a poet and short-story writer and author of public radio commentaries. He co-founded the Flatwillow Arts and Philosophical Society, an artists' group in central Montana. He is a frequent keynote speaker, panelist, and educator in the fields of agriculture, sustainable food systems, chaos theory and organization design, and marketing.

Jennifer Fallein: Goldie Trout, Jenni's grandmother, was her first teacher. When Jenni didn't seem to have the heart for fishing, she set her up by the river to paint and taught her to scribble in a journal. In 1984, Jenni came to Missoula to teach yoga, but stayed on as a nurse at the Blue Mountain Women's Clinic, and then eventually taught third grade and junior high art and science. She now lives in Dillon with her husband, Roger Dunsmore.

Beth Ferris writes: "My early twenties were spent studying and filming mountain goats in the Swan Mountains of northwest Montana, deep in the wilderness, winter and summer. I learned, literally, that life depends on chopping wood and carrying water. I took on the job of botanist, hiking steep trails up avalanche ravines, collecting plants the goats ate. My poetic life spun out from close observation of animals and plants in Montana's wilderness, from still photography to film-making, producing and writing. What coheres is the connection between the love of the actual, visual image on film and the inner poetic image."

Shaun Gant grew up in Clancy, Montana and studied writing with poet Richard Hugo at the University of Montana. She is the recipient of two National Endowment for the Humanities fellowships. Her poems, plays, and collaborations with visual artists are widely published.

Mark Gibbons lives in Missoula with his wife, Pam; sons, Sean and Cache; and their cat, Smelly (who believes he's a dog). Mark writes: "I've lived in Montana all my life; I'm not sure why, but that's important to me—like family and friends and food are important to me. Of course, poetry is important, too, probably falling somewhere after love and just ahead of beer (by a whisker). Yes, that is silly (I prefer silliness) but once or twice I've gotten serious in a poem: please forgive me."

Randall Gloege writes: "I evolved from wanting to become a nuclear engineer to wanting to become and succeeding in becoming an English professor. I lost dozens of credits in math and science while developing a genuine respect for both of these disciplines. Somewhere in the midst of my confusion, I decided two things: I wanted to write, and I felt an obligation to defend wilderness. I helped lead the campaign to protect several hundred-thousand acres of wilderness in south-central Montana—the Absaroka-Beartooth Wilderness."

Patricia Goedicke was the author of twelve books of poetry, the most recent of which, *As Earth Begins to End*, was recognized by the American Library Association as one of the top ten poetry books of the year 2000. As a nationally acclaimed poet, Patricia received many awards and honors. She taught in the Creative Writing Program at the University of Montana for twenty-five years.

Kevin Goodan writes: "My life in Montana (firefighting, ranchwork, fishing) taught me to pay close attention to the details of the natural world, which is the foundation of the work I do in poetry. Writing allows me to go back to my grandparents' ranch across from the airport in Missoula, which is now an industrial park and subdivision, and live once more among that hard-won beauty. I can walk through my grandmother's meticulous plum orchard, listening to the me-yaws of peacocks beneath the poplars she planted when she and my grandfather were young, or ride once more with grandfather on his combine through the dust-bitten days of harvest."

Henrietta Goodman writes: "Perhaps because Montana had been, at first, so foreign, I observed it with a foreigner's eye for detail, and I found myself noticing, and using in my work, the various textures of snow, the behavior of forest fires, the smell of cottonwoods. I became fascinated by extremes of weather, and by the ways that we often allow, even instigate, the greatest upheavals in our personal lives when the weather subjects us to a week of sub-zero temperatures or fires that turn the sun red and the sky dark at mid-day. I began an ongoing series of poems spoken in the persona of a grown-up version of Gretel, from the story of *Hansel and Gretel*. This voice appealed to me because Gretel was, after all, lost in a big wood with nothing to rely on but brotherly love and her own ingenuity; in other words, she was not so different from me."

Loren Graham was born and raised in Broken Arrow, Oklahoma. He studied as a writer and composer at Oklahoma Baptist University, and he took the M.A. in English from Baylor University and the M.F.A. in Poetry from the University of Virginia. He has since taught creative writing at Lynchburg College in Virginia, James Madison University, and Hollins University. He now teaches at Carroll College in Helena.

Jennifer Greene lives on the Flathead Reservation where she was born and raised. She is Salish and Chippewa/Cree and is an enrolled member of the Confederated Salish and Kootenai tribe. She holds a master's degree in English and teaches full-time at Salish Kootenai College in Pablo. Jennifer is married and has three children. Her book, *What I Keep*, won the 1998 First Book Award for Poetry from the Native Writers Circle of the Americas. Jennifer is currently working on a novel.

Sid Gustafson lives with his children Connor and Nina in Bozeman where he writes and also practices his natural approach to veterinary medicine. He is the author of the novels *Prisoners of Flight, Horses They Rode,*and *Lameness in Horses* as well as the guidebook, *First Aid for the Active Dog*. Dr. Gustafson is Professor of Equine Studies at the University of Montana-Western (Dillon) where he directs the Natural Horsemanship Program.

Tami Haaland, the granddaughter of homesteaders, grew up near the Marias River in central Montana. She learned to ride horses and motorcycles, to play the saxophone and piano, to garden and drive a grain truck. Her first collection of poetry, *Breath in Every Room*, won the Nicholas Roerich Prize from Story Line Press. She teaches creative writing at Montana State University-Billings and has spent the past two years investigating the history of poetry in Montana.

Ann White Haggett taught first grade for 26 years in Whitefish and at Starr School on the Blackfeet Reservation. She raised three children on the outskirts of Glacier National Park. Her grandfather built a hardware store in Belt, Montana during the coal mining heydays of the late 1800s, and he recounted to Ann tales of frontier mischief and adventure. Ann's parents made Bozeman home, but the family spent summer weekends in the 30s and 40s camping on the Gallatin River. Her dad's bear deterrent technique at Specimen Creek Campground was two pan lids banged together at the tent flap when night rummaging noises began. "Poetry is about paying attention," Ann writes. "After all, even the smallest attention to beetles, bear scat, and yellow pine needles connect us to the Montana landscape and the seasonal scheme of life and death." Ann lives in Dillon, Montana where she founded and directs the Dillon Farmers' Market.

John Haines, WW II Navy veteran, homesteaded in Alaska during the years 1947-69. He has published many collections of poetry and taught at many universities, including the University of Montana. His most recent collections of poetry are *For the Century's End, Poems 1990-99* (University of Washington Press), and *Of Your Passage, O Summer: Uncollected Poems from the 1960s* (Limberlost Press).

Robin Hamilton raises his son on reverently killed elk and deer, hikes to mountain lakes, and sometimes wins his age group in road races, triathlons, and cross-country ski races. He taught in Montana public schools for thirty-two years, the last twenty-four at Hellgate High School in Missoula where he was English Department Chair until he retired in 2002. Two years later Robin was elected to the Montana House of Representatives. Although his busy political career limits his writing time, he's at work on a novel and more poems.

Matthew Hansen first traveled to the Rocky Mountain Front when he was four and a half months old and belonged to the country for the rest of his young life. He grew up in Missoula, Montana, and graduated in history from the University of Montana in 1982. His interest in oral history led him to write a monograph of the Métis, who settled the South Fork of the Teton River, and to record for the Montana Historical Society the oral histories of those who mined, ranched, or logged in early Montana. His poems are published in a chapbook, *Clearing*. He died of lymphoma in 1984 at 23 years of age.

Jim Harrison, a widely published poet and novelist, divides the year between Montana and Arizona. His most recent works are a novel, *Returning to Earth* (Grove Press) and a book of poetry, *Saving Daylight* (Copper Canyon Press).

Claire Hibbs lives outside of Arlee, Montana where she regularly encounters bears, coyotes and cows on the dirt road winding up the canyon to her home. She was educated at Dartmouth College and at the University of Montana, where she received an MFA in Creative Writing. She has taught in Oakland, California, on the Navajo Nation, and at the University of Montana. She is passionate about giving all children the opportunity to attain an excellent education regardless of economic or cultural background and has worked as a Program Design Specialist for Teach for America. Though the politics of inequity in public education pre-occupy her work-life, she also enjoys motherhood, playing in the outdoors and writing poetry.

John Holbrook writes: "I share a cheerful home in Missoula with my wife Judith of 37 years and our two cats, a recently constructed custom green house (made with recycled commercial awning frames!), two vegetable gardens, spans of flower beds, and two apple trees with a total of 35 different cultivars I've grafted onto them over the last 25 years."

Krys Holmes grew up in eastern Montana, graduated from Rocky Mountain College, and drove her VW bug to Alaska where she worked as a reporter for the *Anchorage Times*. She wrote corporate newsletters for a jet and helicopter company that flew her through polar bear country and onto at-sea oil platforms; ran a dry-goods store in Talkeetna; worked as a freelancer for *National Fisherman* and *Seafood International* magazines, and generally frittered her youth away in the sub-arctic boreal forests where she built a 12 x 16-foot cabin on the shores of Talkeetna Lake. She currently is writing a Montana history textbook for middle-schoolers and writes book reviews for *Montana Magazine*.

Brynn Holt writes: "I was born in 1965 in Deer Lodge, Montana. By the time I was four I had met Andy Warhol, seen Jim Morrison, the L.A. freeways, the Berkeley riots, and had run naked with a pack of dogs in the Arizona desert. I graduated from Helena High in 1984 and received a B.A from The Evergreen State College in Olympia, Washington, in 1993. I have worked in the building trades my entire adolescent and adult life. One of my first poems was published as a family Thanksgiving invitation when I was in third grade. Since then I've published poems in various reviews and journals. Words on paper tell me they are poems; 'No,' I tell them, 'you are words on paper.'"

Richard Hugo's early poems grew out of his love for the lakes, rivers and oceans of the Pacific Northwest where he lived until he was 40. His next home became Missoula, Montana, where he moved to teach creative writing at the University of Montana from 1964 to 1982. In these years, the Montana landscape and its people became the subject of his many poems, as did those of Italy and Scotland where he spent a Fulbright year and then a Guggenheim year. From 1978 to 1982, he was the editor for the Yale Younger Poets Series. His complete poems are published in *Making Certain It Goes On* (W.W. Norton). He died of leukemia in 1982, just short of his 58th birthday.

Lowell Jaeger writes: "I enjoy bringing poetry to all sorts of people, young and old, schooled or not, yea-sayers and nay-sayers. Across the back roads of Montana, I read and teach in communities where folks tell me they've never heard live poetry before. At least they can't recall. And what do I hope my poems say? What do I teach? Each of our lives is part of a greater whole. We are threads in a common cloth, no matter how separate we feel. Poems have spoken this same message throughout time, around the globe. In part, my story is your story. And yours, mine. We share our poems to discover who we are." Lowell teaches creative writing courses at Flathead Valley Community College (Kalispell).

Jack Jelinski has been wandering with a fly rod through wild places for fifty years. He has worked as a Peace Corps volunteer in the Dominican Republic, handyman, pulp-cutter, well-driller, and lifeguard. He is Professor Emeritus of Spanish Literature at Montana State University-Bozeman.

Judith Johnson was resident poet in various schools for the Missoula Writing Collaborative, and she has worked for Common Ground, a program for teenagers. She served as principal for Words With Wings, a grade school summer writing camp, and she has taught writing workshops to diverse audiences. Currently Judith teaches in the Davidson Honors College-University of Montana, has two great-granddaughters and two cats, and is easily mollified by chocolate.

Danell Jones writes: "I grew up in a land of alfalfa farms, dirt bikes, rattlesnakes, one-gas-station towns, and big sky. After a stint as a high school teacher, I left the West to go to graduate school at Columbia. For a decade, I learned to be a New Yorker. By the time I left, I was pretty good at it. In the mid-nineties, I came to Montana to teach English literature and have stayed in the West ever since."

Greg Keeler has taught writing at Montana State University-Bozeman since 1975. He has published six collections of poetry and also writes musical comedies and satirical songs. His works have been aired on Garrison Keillor's *Writers' Almanac, Bob Dobbs Hour of Slack, Dr. Demento, The Car Guys* on NPR, *The Great American Outdoors* on ESPN, and *Subdivide and Conquer*, a documentary on urban sprawl. Keeler has also published a memoir, *Waltzing With The Captain*, (about his experiences with Richard Brautigan).

Joanna Klink is the author of *They Are Sleeping*. Her second book, *Circadian*, is forthcoming from Penguin in 2007. A recipient of a Rona Jaffe Writer's Award in 2003, she teaches poetry at the University of Montana.

Rebecca Knotts' award winning poems have appeared in numerous journals. She teaches literature and writing at the University of Montana-Western (Dillon). She compares her life in Montana to a tapestry: "I can follow the red threads through my child hands picking chokecherries along the Prickly Pear in Wolf Creek. The thread continues to the shotgun, a cabin painted in my grandfather's blood. I follow the yellow thread, light that danced across body and water, children floating on waves in the Missouri, to the roses we placed on my brother's unsettled grave. I follow the blue waves of my Irish mother's fairy songs to the open sky of Great Falls, the blur of geese, wing, and wind. These are a few of my stories. The landscape has her own to tell. I'm learning from her that every creek bed, chokecherry, cottonwood, or Chinook wind, contains what has been buried and birthed."

Alison Kreiss writes: "Born and raised in Seattle, I was drawn to Montana by greed and misanthropy: more wilderness, fewer people. For the past decade, I have crisscrossed this state of mythical exile, spending six years of post-collegiate languor in Missoula, followed by a brief neo-primitive pioneer experiment in a yurt in the Yaak, to my present home in Dillon, where I live with my wilderness-guide husband and wild toddler son."

Melissa Kwasny is the author of two books of poetry, *Thistle* (Lost Horse Press 2006, Winner of the Idaho Prize) and *The Archival Birds* (Bear Star Press 2000); two novels, *Trees Call for What They Need* and *Modern Daughters and the Outlaw West*; and she edited *Toward the Open Field: Poets on the Art of Poetry 1800-1950* (Wesleyan University Press 2004). She lives outside Jefferson City, Montana.

Ed Lahey was born and raised in Butte, and has been writing poetry for fifty years. Ed has taught high school and has worked on mining and pipeline operations and in the trucking business. He also taught at the University of Montana and at Carroll College (Helena). He writes, he says, in order to keep track of himself. His book, *Blind Horses and Other Poems*, won the Montana Art Council's First Book Award for 1979.

Robert Lee earned an MFA from the University of Montana Creative Writing Program. He retired from the Postal Service "without ever going postal," and now works for the Missoula Writing Collaborative. He is the author of *Guiding Elliot*, a novel.

Richard Littlebear writes: "My grandmother used to call the comic books we read 'lazy-making' books because they took so much of our time that we neglected to bring in water, empty the slop bucket, or gather firewood. She stopped calling them that when she got so caught up in one of the stories that she neglected to cook the meal. I have been fascinated by the written word ever since. I once heard an uncle of mine remark that I could chop wood and read a novel at the same time. I wasn't quite that good, but a book was always nearby." Richard earned a doctorate from Boston University in 1994. He returned to the Northern Cheyenne Reservation in 1996, where he is President of Chief Dull Knife College. "Despite my success in the world of white man's education, I learned to read and write the Cheyenne language, and this I consider my greatest academic achievement."

Franco Littlelight, a Montana State University-Billings graduate, currently resides on the Crow Indian Reservation and works for the Crow Head Start Program. He is an enrolled member of the Crow tribe and has made a commitment to working for his people. He has traveled extensively throughout the United States and Canada to visit many Indian reservations. When winter lifts, he leaves his beloved land and people behind to experience other lands and people. Upon his return, he spends the winter telling tales of his exploits, maybe writing some down.

Gary Lundy taught literature and creative writing in New York and Virginia and has been a faculty member at the University of Montana-Western (Dillon) since 1991. He is a widely published poet. He says poetry "gives permission to those who remain outside, who reside in the margins of both the page and the world. Poetry celebrates not only the world as experienced, but also the world as it might be experienced."

Eve Malo writes: "A tragedy in our family, the killing of my grandmother by my uncle, strangely gifted me as a young child with a sense of adventure. My mother's grieving led us to England and Europe. As she grieved by study and travel, she found excellent boarding schools for me where I was exposed to many languages and enjoyed a rainbow of cultures. During W.W. II, we sojourned in every corner of the United States, and again I tasted a smorgasbord of schools, twelve in twelve years. People ask, 'Where are you from?' I answer, 'I am citizen of this magnificent planet.'" In 2007, Eve Malo received the Montana Governor's Humanities Award.

Sophie Mays is in her mid fifties and is the second youngest fluent speaker of the Salish Language. She taught Salish language classes at Salish Kootenai College from 1995-2002. She was then recruited by the Salish language immersion school, Nkwusm, where she taught Salish language to young children. Sophie is now employed by the Native American Language Teacher Training Institute and is excited to teach highly motivated students with a passion for learning Salish.

Joseph R. McGeshick was born in Poplar in 1960. He is of Chippewa and Assiniboine-Sioux heritage. He is an enrolled member of the Sokaogon Chippewa of Mole Lake, Wisconsin. He has taught Native American Studies at Montana State University-Bozeman, Washington State University-Pullman, Fort Peck Community College and Rocky Mountain College. He writes and lives in Pony, Montana.

Wally McRae's first poetry performance was in 1940 at the one room school house up the Rosebud Creek from his family's ranch. He was four years old. He has been an invited performer at all 23 Elko Cowboy Poetry Gatherings and was keynote speaker at the 10th. He is a founding member of the Coal and Cattle Country Players theater group in his hometown and has been involved in nineteen of that group's productions. Wally has received the Governor's Award for the Arts, a Heritage Fellowship from the National Endowment for the Arts, as well as the H.G. Merriam Award from the Mansfield Library at the University of Montana. He is a cattle rancher, south of Colstrip, Montana, where his family has a cow-calf operation.

Maxwell Milton was born in Oakland, California, in 1947. As a teen he spent a number of summers near the Missouri River north of Helena. He has called Helena home since the mid 1970s.

Irvin Moen, a Flathead Valley native, enjoyed rock climbing and sky-diving, but his real passion was poetry. He was a prolific poet, and his hard-hitting poetry ranged from brutally honest love lyrics to political outrage and spiritual meditations. He also wrote about mental illness and his experiences with mental health workers and institutions. Before his death in 2005, he had written hundreds of poems and published dozens in various literary journals.

Carol Douglas Muir is a third generation Montanan from a ranch in Wheatland County where, she says, "the sky truly is big." She has traveled and lived coast to coast and earned degrees from Russell Sage College and Portland State University. Back in Montana for fifteen years now, she currently resides in Missoula with her son's cat.

Bob Muth writes: "If I want to get close to a whitetail deer grazing in our barnyard, I have learned to avert my eyes and advance on a diagonal. So too, as for biography, I must tell you this: On a cold, February morning in 1986, our eighteen year old daughter, Denise, died in an automobile accident. Words collapsed on themselves into black holes of emptiness and need. Poetry was the only opening in the curtain I could find to distill a certain sense of rightness out of the darkness." Bob teaches sixth grade in Columbia Falls.

M.J. Nealon writes: "I've worked as a nurse for 30 years and lived in many states, but no place created the sense of tranquility I felt when I first came to Montana in my twenties. I felt I had found my way home, though I continued to work as a traveling nurse, moving frequently. I also wrote poems. Everywhere I lived, I looked for the right words. Words made a kind of home I could take with me."

Brenda Nesbitt lived with her husband and two children in a cabin inside the forests of northwest Montana beyond the reach of electricity and other conveniences. For many years, Brenda commuted more than 60 miles each way to attend classes part-time at Flathead Valley Community College in Kalispell. Eventually, through a distance-learning program, she earned a degree from Norwich University. She was accepted into the Graduate Creative Writing Program at the University of Montana, and was killed in a car accident while en route to Missoula during her first semester in 1996.

Rick Newby, a native of Kalispell, was raised in Helena and Billings. He is the executive director of Drumlummon Institute, a nonprofit enterprise dedicated to fostering research, writing, and publishing on the culture of Montana and the American West, and editor of *Drumlummon Views*, an online journal devoted to Montana arts and culture (www.drumlummon.org). Trained as a poet at the University of Montana, Rick Newby is the author of four collections of poems, including *A Radiant Map of the World* which won of the Montana Arts Council's First Book Award for 1981.

Sheryl Noethe is the artistic director of the Missoula Writing Collaborative, a passionate teacher, and an advocate for poetry. She is author (with Jack Collom) of *Poetry Everywhere*, an innovative textbook with emphasis on "writing as an adventure and words as the building blocks of joy and discovery." She believes dreams are where universes connect. She and her husband live at the foot of Mount Jumbo with a motley line of beloved rescued animals, including a bloodhound named Peaches and a one-eyed feral cat named Mike Tyson.

Ed Noonan, Executive Director of the Myrna Loy Center for the Media and Performing Arts (Helena) is also an adjunct professor of Film, Communications, and

Performing Arts at Carroll College. *Warren Street House*, a play dealing with a group home for the developmentally disabled, was performed off-Broadway at the Harold Clurman Theater in 1994. His play *Taking History* won an Individual Artists Fellowship from the Montana Arts Council. A collection of his poetry, *Noisy Soil*, was published in 1998 by Bedrock Books.

Elnora A. Old Coyote writes: "I am the eldest of six children raised on a homestead south of Laurel, Montana until drought, then grasshoppers, then Mormon crickets cleaned us out, and we left the dryland homestead. We went through poverty years but never missed school. Maybe I've spent more years in school as a student and as a teacher than any Montanan ever. Wallace Stegner made a search for the characteristics of a Westerner. I believe I'm one—born and raised in the rainshadow of the Rocky Mountains, able to spend hours alone anywhere, healthier than average, energy to spare, able to solve problems, resourceful and creative."

Greg Owens is a playwright, poet, and songwriter who lives in Bozeman. His plays, *The Life and Times of Tulsa Lovechild* and *Home Front*, were published by Broadway Play Publishing. His writing was also included in the *Best Stage Monologues 2005* anthology from Smith & Kraus. Greg's work has been read and performed in New York, London, Chicago, and Los Angeles. He teaches Creative Writing at Montana State University and volunteers with the Bozeman High School Speech and Theatre programs.

Robert Pack is author of eighteen books of poetry and numerous books of essays and criticism. He teaches courses in Shakespeare, Romantic Poetry, Modern Poetry, Creative Writing, Visions of Nature, and Ways of Knowing at the Honors College of the University of Montana-Missoula. He and his wife, Patty, live in a log home with a panoramic view of the Rocky Mountains in Condon, Montana.

Elsie Pankowski writes: "Poetry was first introduced to me in a one-room country school. While reading nineteenth-century poets, I complained to the teacher about the archaic language, and she challenged me to write something better. I still have that first effort about a colorful prairie sunset. I wrote poems while doing chores, composing them on horseback and reciting them to my mare's questioning ears. I've had two books and several hundred poems published and won Montana's Mary Brennan Clapp Award five times."

Greg Pape writes: "I had been spending parts of summers fishing and exploring the mountains in previous years, and I had had a correspondence with Dick Hugo, so when the opportunity to teach at University of Montana came along it seemed like great good fortune. Marnie and I drove up from Florida with all our belongings, stored our stuff, and spent our first week or so living in a tent on Rock Creek. We found a house to rent up the Bitterroot, which we later bought, and started a family. I still love teaching, and I am writing poems and prose, and trying to follow Hugo's lead in making certain it goes on."

Amy Ratto Parks writes: "Within a mile of my childhood home in Cincinnati were two major interstates, a main railroad line, a General Motors plant, the US Playing Card Company, and five churches. During my freshman year of college I realized that I wanted to leave—I hadn't been too many places out west, but for some reason (and who knows where I heard it) I was fascinated by the words, 'Missoula, Montana.' It has certainly been a place where we've found solid roots. There are days when I find myself making two toddler lunch plates, wondering whether the winter's snowfall will feed the rivers all summer, and trying to revise the title to a new poem all at once, and I am aware of how 'Missoula' our lives have become. Thank God, I think next. Thank God."

Carol Foussard Peck grew up in the dry land wheat country of north central Montana. She is a graduate of the College of Great Falls and the Columbus Hospital School of Medical Technology. She works as a Clinical Laboratory Scientist at Barrett Hospital and Health Care in Dillon. Diagnosed with cancer in her early forties, Carol asked herself some of the big questions such as, "What have I always wanted to do that I have not yet done?" One of the answers was, "write poetry." Carol enjoys the sense of discovery that comes from finding just the right metaphor to more deeply express a truth or an emotion.

Gwen Petersen's warm-hearted ranch woman's humor has won applause and acclaim at the National Cowboy Poetry Gathering in Elko, Nevada. A working rancher for over thirty years, she now raises miniature horses. She lives near Big Timber, Montana.

Carolyn Pettit Pinet writes: "Sometimes I get up in the morning, look at the mountains and wonder how I got here! I was born in Wales, the land of song, rugby, and poetry, and heard my first poems from my mother who had the intuition of a Welsh witch. My other interests include Argentine tango. Both tango and poetry embody the paradox of 'alone-together.' The tango dancer must work on the intricate figures alone, but always with a partner in mind. Poetry too is a solitary practice, but it reaches out to others—to amuse, provoke, console, exhilarate, move—whatever catches the imagination in the moment."

Henry Real Bird, Baucheewuchaitchish, was born on the Crow Indian Reservation and raised in the traditions of the Upsauloeka, the Crow. From the rising sun over the Wolf Teeth Mountains, to the noon day sun over the Mountain With Something Beyond, till the sun sets behind Shot Boulder Mountain, he listens for whispers in the pines under the uncountable stars. Through happiness, sadness, heartache, triumph, defeat, struggle, racism, conversation, peace, turmoil, he wanders in thought, searching for poems. He has written twelve books for children and three books of poetry. Henry teaches at Northern Cheyenne Tribal School and raises bucking horses on Yellow Leggins Creek, between the Little Big Horn River, and Rosebud Creek. He enjoys putting his grandchildren on horses and checking fences to make sure the mares have grass and water.

Lois Red Elk writes: "My dad and I were very close, and we often conversed about our dual lives as tribal people co-existing with the dominant society. He advised me to be a good earth-walker. 'The earth has all kinds of stories (poems) to share with anyone who wants to listen.' But, he said, we need to listen with our eyes and our spirit. He said it's complicated listening with just our ears. 'We are earth-walkers and in order to live with the earth we have to listen to her.' In one of my lives I am afforded the luxury and excitement of traveling to meet and work with the artists of other tribes on their homelands, in their beautiful environments and listen to their profound cultural stories and songs. I've listened carefully. My poems reflect what I've seen, felt and heard. Predominantly my work reflects the positive and beautiful. But, in order to convey the whole story of our lives, I also write about the harsh and disturbing."

Steven Ray Robbins writes: "I grew up in Butte Montana. Atypical to my generation, I was conscious always of my family traditions which were creative in nature. I grew to love the arts under the mentorship of Mary Keene, Joe Antinoli, and the Montana poet, Edward Lahey. My soul is rooted in the creative arts and a deep spiritual awareness of the divine. I am humbled by being here at the State Hospital where I have received superb care and share in the nurturing of what I call affectionately the old crowd. I have created a new poetic form which I have dubbed the Vladvostok sonnet, based on the French rondelet."

Katherine Romano began writing poetry out of necessity; chronic back pain made writing prose a luxury. She has spent her last decade working for environmental protection and grassroots media. A native New Yorker, Katherine is "still learning from Montanans how to take it easy, keep my priorities straight, and connect with the ancient wisdom of the planet."

Sheila Ruble teaches poetry and photography workshops for the Billings-based Writer's Voice program. Besides poetry, she writes non-fiction magazine articles, teaches dressage lessons and serves as an instructor for Beartooth Pony Club. She has run the 4-H dog obedience program for Yellowstone County since 1975. Her favorite activities include exploring back roads in eastern Montana, working with her horses, and spending time at the Ruble's cabin in the West Boulder Valley.

Charles M. Russell (1864-1926) of Great Falls, Montana, known as "The Cowboy Artist," is little regarded for his poetry. However, he wrote over 70 verses, most of which accompanied gifts of art works. The poem printed here, in its original version, was written on a watercolor painting titled "The Fool and The Knight," which depicts an encounter in the English woods. Completed after an April 1914 trip to England for an exhibition of his work, the painting was a Christmas gift to his neighbors, the Albert Trigg family. The threat of WWI was heavy in the air, and Charlie's return trip was aboard the Lusitania, which was sunk a year later by a German U-boat.

June Billings Safford, a native of Brooklyn, New York, found her first "real home" on a small working ranch near Bozeman, the Bar Double J, with horses, rabbits, chickens, geese, and a 600 pound sow, Missy. For many years she taught creative writing courses at Bozeman High School. She is also a painter.

Ripley Schemm was born in Michigan in 1929 and raised in Great Falls, Montana. After teaching back east for 20 years, she returned in 1973 to Montana with her two children, Matthew and Melissa, and married Richard Hugo. She taught literature and creative writing at the University of Montana and worked for 12 years for the Montana Poets In The Schools program. Her early poems are published in a chapbook, *Mapping My Father*. In 2003, The University of Nebraska Press published *Writing For Her Life*, Ripley's biography of her mother, novelist Mildred Walker. Her collection of poetry, *In The Hands of Their History*, is from Cedar House Books.

Rob Schlegel earned an MFA from the University of Montana where he now teaches writing courses. His manuscript *Iceblink* was a finalist for the 2005 New California Poetry Series. His poems and reviews have appeared or are forthcoming in *AGNI*, *Barrowstreet, The Boston Review, VOLT* and elsewhere.

Brandon Shimoda curates the New Lakes Reading and Performance Series in

Missoula, and helps edit *CutBank* and *Octopus Magazine*. Educated at Sarah Lawrence College and the University of Montana, where he was a Poetry Fellow, he is also the recipient of an AWP Intro Award and an LEAW Fellowship from the Virginia Center for the Creative Arts. His poems have appeared in journals such as *Hayden's Ferry Review* and *New Orleans Review*.

Deborah Slicer's book *The White Calf Kicks* won the 2003 Autumn House Prize, which was judged by Naomi Shihab Nye. As a Montana resident, Deborah says her poems are "inspired by the landscapes and animals with whom I share this brief life."

Marie Smith was born in 1927, raised in the West Australian bush and on the shores of the Indian Ocean. She moved in 1952 to marry Idaho rancher/cowboy artist, Cecil Smith (1910-1984). She has ranched, raised eleven children, taught school, lived in four western states (Montana since 1972) and performed her work in seven states, Canada and Australia. Inducted into the Cowboy Poets of Idaho Hall of Fame in 1996 and nominated Female Poet of the Year by the Academy of Western Artists in 1997, her work may be found in three of her own volumes, most recently *Exchanging Courtesies*, and numerous collections of western poetry. In her 80th year she still writes daily.

M.L. Smoker belongs to the Assiniboine and Sioux tribes of the Fort Peck Reservation in northeastern Montana. Her family's home is on Tabexa Wakpa (Frog Creek), a traditional camping ground for the Assiniboine people. She holds an MFA from the University of Montana-Missoula, where she was the recipient of the Richard Hugo Fellowship. Her first collection of poems, *Another Attempt at Rescue*, was published by Hanging Loose Press in the spring of 2005. M.L. Smoker currently resides in Helena, Montana, where she works for the Office of Public Instruction, in the Indian Education Division.

Jim Soular writes: "My best friend was killed in Vietnam, right before my eyes, and my life veered forever as though I had been broadsided by a truck. One day in 1986, after a particularly dark stretch of many dark stretches, a friend suggested I write a poem about those monsoon memories. I read the poems of Richard Hugo late one night way up the drainage where I lived alone near Superior, Montana, and I allowed myself to be drawn into the words, the images, the landscapes." Jim received an MFA from the Creative Writing Program at the University of Montana in 1992. He is the Writing Lab instructor at Flathead Valley Community College (Kalispell) where he also teaches composition and literature courses.

David Spencer was influenced early on by his poet and historian grandmother in a home "brimming over with books." For many years he studied and traveled abroad, including two solo bicycle pilgrimages from the Alps to the Greek archipelago. He earned a degree in 1990 from Carroll College and lives in Helena. He enjoys a "still-ongoing relationship with the truly extraordinary Holter Museum of Art, which—all hyperbole aside—[he] regards as both the Uffizi of the Northern Rockies & the heART chakra/hub of Helena where the spokes of what by any standard is a remarkable community converge."

Shirley Steele has taught poetry classes at Eastern Montana College and Rocky Mountain College. She served as Writers Chair for the Billings Arts Association and State Writers Chair for the Montana Institute of the Arts. In 1992 she was presented the Montana Governor's Award for Distinguished Achievement in the Arts. She says, "I write any place and every place; I don't need a special place. I write while I'm working around the house or yard, in the car (at a stoplight!), while my husband fishes, and in the dark in the middle of the night."

Malcolm "Mac" Swan writes: "During my teens and early 20s, I worked on an isolated ranch in Southwest Montana. I wrote letters home, and when responses were slow in coming, I scribbled stories and poems, clinging to some sense of connection to the larger world. Writing for me has always been about staying connected. I enjoy discovering what I'm thinking in words. After earning a teaching degree from the University of Montana, I intended to sail the Pacific, but my truck needed fixing so I looked for temporary work near my parents' home in Polson. That teaching job lasted 28 years. Along the way, I married a beautiful woman, raised two children, and wrote a book about Montana writers."

David Thomas grew up in north-central Montana and enrolled in the University of Montana hoping to pursue a military career. The Vietnam War led him to abandon this ambition and seek an alternative fortune which led him to the streets of Seattle and San Francisco where he "picked up the trail of his beatnik literary forebears." David lives and works in Missoula, Montana.

Jo Anne Salisbury Troxel spent her youth on the Flathead Reservation near Arlee, Montana. "We lived in a $39.00 shack on ten acres with Finley Creek on one side and the railroad track on the other. When the four o'clock troop train blew its whistle through the town, I would drop my fishing pole and run across the pasture to wave at the boys. The train slowed near the depot, and the recruits waved and yelled, sometimes tossed me candy. I even got marriage proposals: 'Marry me, Sweetheart…I'll be back!' I was ten years old." Troxel is a retired high school teacher and a human rights activist in the Gallatin Valley.

Lowell Uda is interim pastor at Clancy United Methodist Church in Clancy, Montana. He received a Bachelor of Arts degree in English from the University of Utah in 1962, a Master of Fine Arts degree in Creative Writing from the University of Iowa Writers' Workshop in 1967, and a Master of Divinity degree from The Iliff School of Theology in 1993. He has taught literature and writing at the University of Hawaii and the University of Montana and, as an ordained elder in the United Methodist Church, convened creative writing and spiritual formation groups open to church members and the general public at each of the churches he served.

Michael Umphrey served as the Executive Director of the Montana Heritage Project. His first book of poems, *The Lit Window,* was published by the Cleveland State University Poetry Center, and his second, *The Breaking Edge,* won the Merriam-Frontier Award and was published by the University of Montana. Michael runs the ambulance service on the Flathead Reservation. He makes his home in St. Ignatius.

Karen Volkman was born in Miami and received her B.A. from New College in Sarasota, Florida, and an M.A. from Syracuse University. Her first book, *Crash's Law,* was a National Poetry Series selection, published by W.W. Norton in 1996. Her second book, *Spar,* received the Iowa Poetry Prize and the 2002 James Laughlin Award · from the Academy of American Poets. She currently lives in the lower Rattlesnake in Missoula and teaches on the MFA faculty at the University of Montana.

David Waldman earned a degree in art from Montana State University. He is a noted painter. "Polio left my right arm paralyzed at the age of two. That wired me apart from my blue collar roots. Artists and writers accepted me, helped me, excited me." Waldman lives in Bozeman.

Luanne "Annie" Tillery Waldow and her husband live on a small farm north of Culbertson. "On our farm," Luanne writes, "you'll find wheat fields burning in the Montana sun, oats crisping in the summer heat, Buelingo cattle, Angus X cattle, chickens, dogs, turkeys, ducks, North American Curly horses, Appaloosa horses, and a pony or two." She teaches in an elementary school and works as an advocate for the special needs of children from rural areas and reservations.

Jack Waller retired years ago to a life of creative and contemplative poverty centered around daily practices of writing, music, and making furniture. In 2005, he celebrated— as a newlywed and first-time father—his sixty-third birthday. He lives in Virginia City with his wife Kristin, daughter Ruby, and good dog Boji. He has been a poet and autobiographer for over forty years.

Kelly Weaver was born in Helena, and grew up bucking bales and learning how to work. She writes: "I left home when I was 17 and traveled in the states and Mexico for a couple decades. Ended up in Seeley Lake, Montana with four-year-old twins and taking care of my folks. I have always needed the water and the woods around me. I find a great deal of inspiration and sometimes the peace I seek there. I filled dozens of notebooks and never kept any of it, till one day it meant something to someone else. I didn't write my poems, they wrote me."

Emily Wecker: Although deep inside she is surely a romantic (and somewhat depressed) poet, she also enjoys listening to rock bands, playing pinball, watching skateboarders being attacked by cats, and intimidating people who are at least a foot taller than she. "Just because I write poetry doesn't mean that I have no sense of humor or an obsession with typical female issues," she says. Having turned fifteen, Emily concludes she has arrived at the best part of her life now that she's finally out of middle school.

James Welch was born in Browning, Montana, of Blackfeet and Gros Ventre heritage. He attended schools on the Blackfeet and Fort Belknap reservations. He received a BA from the University of Montana in 1965, then spent two years in the MFA program, studying under the acclaimed poet, Richard Hugo. *Riding the Earthboy 40* was his first and only book of poems. He wrote one book of non-fiction and five novels, including *Fools Crow*, which won the Los Angeles Times Book Award for Fiction. Among his many awards, he won a Montana Governor's Award in 1981, a Lifetime Achievement Award of the Native Writers Circle in 1997. In 2000 the French government made him a Chevalier de l'Ordre des arts et des letters.

Elizabeth H. Wood is a writer in Roundup, Montana. Born in the San Francisco Bay Area, educated at San Francisco State University, Elizabeth left the city she loves and moved with her partner Wilbur Wood to Roundup, Montana, in 1971 to have a garden in her own backyard. She is a theater director, script writer, editor, supporter of local artists, and advocate for clean renewable energy and local food for all of Montana.

Wilbur Wood grew up roaming the mountains and high plains of central Montana, earned graduate and post-graduate degrees from the University of Montana and San Francisco State, and with his partner Elizabeth Hughes Wood has co-hosted writer-artist groups from San Francisco to central Montana. Wilbur lives in Roundup. He is a poet, essayist, journalist, editor, gardener, renewable energy activist, and currently on the board of Montana Arts Council.

Paul Zarzyski, forged by his iron ore miner father, Len, and tempered by his Italian mother, Dee, in Hurley, Wisconsin, pulled into Missoula in the Fall of '73—still pronouncing his *th*'s like *d*'s— to study with his maestro-for-life, Dick Hugo. Since then, he's spent a dozen years riding bucking horses, has been featured at 22 annual Cowboy Poetry Gatherings in Elko, Nevada, has received the Montana Governor's Arts Award for Literature, has published 10 books and chapbooks, and has recorded four spoken-word CDs, including, most recently, *Collisions Of Reckless Love* and *Rock 'n' Rowel*. Paul writes west of Great Falls and makes his living as a poet.

Janet Zupan earned an MFA in poetry from the University of Montana in 1996. So far, most of her poems are caged in landscapes shy of the Rockies—among cacti and creosote bushes, between low and high tides, or scratched out of chigger-infested fields. Her poems have most recently appeared in *The Apple Valley Review* and in *Montana Women Writers: A Geography of the Heart*. Her essay, "Vertigo," appeared in *I Thought My Father Was God* (edited by Paul Auster).

Kim Zupan believes every fiction writer's a poet and every poet a fictioneer, and it's all about the sound and the music of the words and making strawmen come alive. He says "Friend Zarzyski owes me big time for leveraging me to cast prose out among the jagged-edged lines of all these fine poets. I'll take pie." Kim's work has appeared in numerous anthologies, including *Hunting's Best Short Stories*, and *The New Montana Story*. In his youth, he worked for several ranches in the Judith Basin and spent a decade riding bareback horses.

Acknowledgements:

Sandra Alcosser: "Cry" © 2000 Sandra Alcosser. Reprinted from *A Fish to Feed All Hunger*, with permission of the author and Ahsahta Press (Boise State University). "The Meadowlark, The Mother" previously appeared in *Parabola Magazine*.

Frederick Bridger: "Remembering a Visit to My Father" previously appeared in *That Thing You Do*.

Ed Chaberek: "Requiem For Louie Z-1994" previously appeared in *Spare Change*.

Madeline DeFrees: "Pendant Watch" © 1978 Madeline DeFrees. Reprinted from *When Sky Lets Go*, with the permission of the author and George Braziller, Inc. "Pendant Watch" also appeared in *Malahat Review*.

Chris Dombrowski: "October Suite" previously appeared in *Crazyhorse*.

Roger Dunsmore: "Dog Spelled Backwards," "Aurora Borealis," "A True War Story," and "Navajo Springs" previously appeared in *Drumlummon Views*.

Mark Gibbons: "Next" © 2007 Mark Gibbons. Reprinted from *blue horizon*, with the permission of the author and Two Dogs Press (Flagstaff, Arizona).

Patricia Goedicke: "Montana Pears" previously appeared in *Montana Women Writers: A Geography of the Heart* (Farcountry Press 2006). Reprinted with permission of Connie Poten.

Henrietta Goodman: "Gretel Alone" © 2007 Henrietta Goodman. Reprinted from *Take What You Want*, with permission of the author and Alice James Books.

Loren Graham: "The Banquet" previously appeared in *Ploughshares*.

Tami Haaland: "Let Deer Come Crashing" previously appeared in *High Desert Journal*.

John Haines: "The Eye In The Rock" © 1993 John Haines. Reprinted from *The Owl in the Mask of the Dreamer*, with permission of the author and Graywolf Press (Saint Paul, Minnesota).

Matthew Hansen: "The Silver Grill Café" © 1986 Matthew Hansen. Reprinted from *Clearing* (Kutenai Press 1986), with permission of Ripley Schemm.

Richard Hugo: "Driving Montana" © 1984 by The Estate of Richard Hugo. Reprinted from *Making Certain It Goes On: Collected Poems of Richard Hugo* by Richard Hugo with permission of Ripley Schemm and W.W. Norton & Company, Inc.

Lowell Jaeger: "Nobody Special," and "We All Know Trouble When We See It" ©
2006 Lowell Jaeger. Reprinted from *Nobody Special*, with the permission of the author
and Pudding House Press (Columbus, Ohio). "How He Cut Himself Shaving" © 2006
Lowell Jaeger. Reprinted from *The Banana Man*, with the permission of the author
and Pudding House Press (Columbus, Ohio). "Together" © Lowell Jaeger. Reprinted
from *Star Crossed*, with the permission of the author and Pudding House Press
(Columbus, Ohio). "Nobody Special" previously appeared in *Atlanta Review*. "Flying
Toad" previously appeared in *CutThroat*. "How He Cut Himself Shaving" previously
appeared in *Poetry*. "Learning to Dance" previously appeared in *Iowa Review*. "Together"
previously appeared in *Red Hawk Review*. "Sin and Salvation" previously appeared in
MO: Writings From the River. "We All Know Trouble When We See It" previously
appeared in *Drumlummon Views*.

Joanna Klink: "Vireo" previously appeared in *The Laurel Review*.

Melissa Kwasny: "Reading Novalis in Montana" previously appeared in *Montana Women
Writers: A Geography of the Heart* (Farcountry Press 2006). Reprinted with permission of
the author. "Reading Novalis in Montana" also appeared in *Willow Springs*.

Wallace McRae: "Riders' Block" © 1992 Wallace McRae. Reprinted from
Cowboy Curmudgeon (Gibb Smith, Publisher)with permission of the author.

Rick Newby: "Night Vigil" © 2002 Rick Newby. Reprinted from *The Suburb of Long
Suffering: Poems and Prose* (Bedrock Editions 2002), with permission of the author.
"Untitled" previously appeared in *Drumlummon Views*.

Elnora A. Old Coyote: "Northeaster in November" © 2000 Elnora A. Old Coyote.
Reprinted from *Cheatgrass and Tumbleweed* (Fenske Companies 2000), with permission
of the author.

Charles M. Russell: "The Fool and The Knight" reprinted from *Regards to The Bunch*
(1992), with permission of the C.M. Russell Museum and Elizabeth Dear.

Elsie Pankowski: "Drilling the Well" © 2003 Elsie Pankowski. Reprinted from
Gathering Stones, with permission of the author and Pudding House Press (Columbus,
Ohio). "Drilling the Well" also appeared in *Amelia*.

Amy Ratto Parks: "Grounding" © 2004 Amy Ratto Parks. Reprinted from *Bread and
Water Body* (University of Montana), with permission of the author.

Carolyn Pettit Pinet: "The Other Woman" previously appeared in *The Oregonian*.

Ripley Schemm: "Anastasia's Afternoon" © 1981Ripley Schemm. Reprinted from
Mapping My Father (Dooryard Press 1981) with permission of the author.

Brandon Shimoda: "*from* Lake M" previously appeared in *Xantippe*.

A List of Books by Montana Poets Represented in This Anthology:

Alcosser, Sandra. *The Blue Vein*. Brighton Press, 2006.
_____*Each Bone a Prayer*. Charles Street Press, 1982.
_____*Except by Nature*. Graywolf Press, 1998.
_____*A Fish to Feed All Hunger*. Ahsahta, 2000.
_____*Glyphs*. Brighton Press, 2001.
_____*Sleeping Inside the Glacier*. Brighton Press, 1997.
_____*A Woman Hit By a Meteor.* Brighton Press, 2001.

Allen, Minerva. *Campfire Stories of the Fort Belknap Community*. Fort Belknap Schools, 1980.
_____ *Like Spirits of the Past Trying to Break Out and Walk to the West.* Wowapi Books, 1974.
_____*Minerva Allen's Indian Cookbook*. Wowapi Books, 1988.
_____*Spirits Rest.* Graphics Art, 1981.
_____*Winter Smoke Poetry*. M.A. Press, 1996.

Blunt, Judy. *Breaking Clean*. Alfred A. Knopf, 2002.
_____*Not Quite Stone.* University of Montana, 1992.

Bradshaw, Pansy. *Best Gay Erotica 1998*. Cleis Press, 1998.
_____*Betty and Pansy's Severe Queer Review of San Francisco*. Cleis Press, 2003.
_____ *Like Counting Teeth*. Running Dog Press, 2007.

Buckley, B.J. *Artifacts: Poems by B.J. Buckley*. Willow Bee Publishing, 1987.
_____*Moonhorses and The Red Bull*. Pronghorn Press, 2005.

Burgess, Philip. *Badlands Child.* Touch of Light Publishing, 2001.

Cahoon, Heather. *Elk Thirst*. University of Montana, 2005.

Chaberek, Ed. *The Berkshire Polish Bar & Other Blue Collar Poems*. Ibbetson St. Press, 1999.
_____ *TYPES*. Superior Poetry Press, 2001.
_____*Voices From A German Graveyard*. Superior Poetry Press, 2007.

Charles, Casey. *Controlled Burn*. Pudding House Press, 2007.
_____ *The Sharon Kowalski Case: Lesbian & Gay Rights on Trial*. University of Kansas
    Press, 2003.

Charlo, Victor. *Swift Current Time*. Charlo Press, 2002.

Dale, David. *Montana Primer*. Big Mountain Publishing, 1996.

_____*Skating Backwards*. Big Mountain Publishing, 1999.

_____*Stumbling Over Stones*. Wright Impressions, 2002.

_____*The Way a Bear Is*. Big Mountain Publishing, 1994.

_____*What We Call Our Own*. Wright Impressions, 1993.

DeFrees, Madeline. *Blue Dusk: New & Collected Poems, 1951-2001*. Copper Canyon Press, 2001.

_____*Double Dutch*. Red Wing Press, 1999.

_____*From the Darkroom*. Bobbs-Merrill, 1964.

_____*Imaginary Ancestors*. Broken Moon Press, 1990.

_____*Later Thoughts from the Springs of Silence*. Bobbs-Merrill, 1962.

_____*The Light Station on Tillamook Rock*. Arrowood Press, 1990.

_____*Springs of Silence*. Prentice-Hall, 1953.

_____*Magpie on the Gallows*. Copper Canyon Press, 1982.

_____*Possible Sibyls*. Lynx House Press, 1991.

_____*Spectral Waves: New & Uncollected Poems*. Copper Canyon Press, 2006.

_____*When Sky Lets Go*. George Braziller, Inc., 1978.

DeMarinis, Rick. *Apocalypse Then*. Seven Stories Press, 2004.

_____*The Art and Craft of the Short Story*. Story Press, 2000.

_____*Borrowed Hearts: New and Selected Stories*. Seven Stories Press, 2000.

_____*The Burning Women of Far Cry*. Arbor House, 1986.

_____*Cinder*. Farrar, Straus, and Geroux, 1978.

_____*A Clod of Wayward Marl*. Dennis McMillan Publications, 2001.

_____*The Coming Triumph of the Free World*. Viking, 1988.

_____*Jack and Jill*. E.P. Dutton, 1979.

_____*A Lovely Monster*. Simon and Schuster, 1975.

_____*The Mortician's Apprentice*. W.W. Norton, 1994.

_____*Scimitar*. E.P. Dutton, 1977.

_____*Sky Full of Sand*. Dennis McMillan Publications, 2003.

_____*Under the Wheat*. University of Pittsburgh Press, 1986.

_____*The Voice of America*. W.W. Norton, 1991.

_____*The Year of the Zinc Penny*. W.W. Norton, 1989.

Dombrowski, Chris. *Midst*. Punctilious Press, 2007.

Dunsmore, Roger. *The Bear Remembers*. Earth's Mind Press, 1990.
_____*Blood House*. Pulp Press, 1987.
_____*Earth's Mind: Essays in Native Literature*. University of New Mexico Press, 1997.
_____*Laszlo Toth*. Pulp Press, 1977.
_____*On the Road to Sleeping Child Hotsprings*. Pulp Press, 1977.
_____*The Sharp-Shinned Hawk*. Blackberry Books, 1987.
_____*Tiger Hill: China Poems*. Camphorweed Press, 2005.

Gant, Shaun. *A Book of Cowgirl Poetry*. Soft Spur Press, 2002.
_____*Morning Poems and 5 a.m. Drawings*. Newtopia, 2003.
_____*Whisk, Lyric, Logic*. Touch of Light Publishing, 2002.

Gibbons, Mark. *blue horizon*. Two Dogs Press, 2007.
_____*Circling Home*. Scattered Cairns Press, 2000.
_____*Connemara Moonshine*. Camphorweed Press, 2002.
_____*Something Inside Us*. Big Mountain Publishing, 1995.

Goedicke, Patricia. *As Earth Begins to End*. Copper Canyon Press, 2000.
_____*Between Oceans*. Harcourt, Brace & World, 1968.
_____*Crossing the Same River*. University of Massachusetts Press, 1980.
_____*The Dog That Was Barking Yesterday*. Lynx House Press, 1980.
_____*For the Four Corners*. Ithaca House, 1976.
_____*Invisible Horses*. Milkweed Editions, 1996.
_____*The King of Childhood*. Confluence Press, 1984.
_____*Listen, Love*. Barnwood Press, 1986.
_____*Paul Bunyan's Bearskin*. Milkweed Editions, 1992.
_____*The Tounges We Speak: New and Selected Poems*. Milkweed Editions, 1989.
_____*The Trail That Turns on Itself*. Ithaca House, 1978.
_____*The Wind of Our Going*. Copper Canyon Press, 1985.

Goodan, Kevin. *In The Ghost House Acquainted*. Alice James Books, 2004.

Goodman, Henrietta. *Take What You Want*. Alice James Books, 2007.

Graham, Loren. *Mose*. Wesleyan University Press, 1994.

Greene, Jennifer. *What I keep*. Greenfield Review Press, 1999.

Gustafson, Sid. *First Aid for the Active Dog*. Alpine Publications, 2003.
_____*Horses They Rode*. Riverbend Publishing, 2006.
_____*Prisoners Of Flight*. The Permanent Press, 2003.

Haaland, Tami. *Breath in Every Room*. Story Line Press, 2001.

Haggett, Ann. *Skating Backwards*. Pudding House Press, 2007.

Haines, John. *Cicada*. Wesleyan University Press, 1977.
_____*Fables And Distances, New & Selected Essays*. Graywolf Press, 1996.
_____*For The Century's End, Poems 1990-99*. University of Washington Press, 2001.
_____*Living Off The Country*. University of Michigan Press, 1981.
_____*New Poems*. Story Line Press, 1990.
_____*Of Your Passage, O Summer*, Limberlost Press, 2004.
_____*The Owl In The Mask of The Dreamer, Collected Poems*. Graywolf Press, 1993.
_____*The Stars, The Snow, The Fire: Twenty-Five Years In the Alaska Wilderness*. Graywolf Press, 1989.
_____*The Stone Harp*. Wesleyan University Press, 1971.
_____*Winter News*. Wesleyan University Press, 1966.

Hansen, Matthew. *Clearing*. The Kutenai Press, 1986.

Harrison, Jim. *After Ikkyu*. Shambhala Centaur Editions, 1996.
_____*The Beast God Forgot to Invent*. Grove Press, 2001.
_____*The Boy Who Ran to the Woods*. Atlantic Monthly Press, 2000.
_____*Braided Creek*. Copper Canyon Press, 2003.
_____*Dalva*. Simon Schuster/Washington Square Press, 1991.
_____*Farmer*. Delta Trade Paperbacks, 1980.
_____*A Good Day to Die*. Random House: Bantam Dell Publishing Group, 1981.
_____*Julip*. Houghton Mifflin, 1995.
_____*Just Before Dark*. Clark City Press, 1991.
_____*Legends of the Fall*. Random House: Bantam Dell Publishing Group, 1980.
_____*Letters To Yesenin*. Sumac Press, 1973.
_____*Locations*. W.W. Norton, 1968.
_____*Off to the Side: A Memoir*. Grove Press, 2002.
_____*Outlyers & Ghazals*. Simon & Schuster, 1971.
_____*Plain Song*. W.W. Norton, 1965.
_____*The Raw & The Cooked*. Grove Press, 2002.
_____*Returning to Earth*. Ithaca House, 1973.
_____*Returning to Earth*. Atlantic Monthly Press, 2007.
_____*The Road Home*. Simon Schuster/Washington Square Press, 1991.
_____*Saving Daylight*. Copper Canyon Press, 2006.
_____*Selected & New Poems*. Delta/Seymour Lawrence, 1989.
_____*The Shape of the Journey*. Copper Canyon Press, 1998.
_____*The Summer He Didn't Die*. Atlantic Monthly Press, 2005.

_____*Sundog*. Random House: Bantam Dell Publishing Group, 1991.

_____*The Theory & Practice of Rivers*. Clark City Press, 1989.

_____*True North*. Grove Press, 2004.

_____*Warlock*. Random House: Bantam Dell Publishing Group, 1982.

_____*Wolf: A False Memoir*. Random House: Bantam Dell Publishing Group, 1981.

_____*The Woman Lit By Fireflies*. Houghton Mifflin, 1991.

Holbrook, John. *Clear Water On The Swan*. SkyHouse Publishers, 1992.

_____*Loose Wool, River Tackle, Pencil Drafts*. Pudding House Press, 2002.

Hugo, Richard. *31 Letters and 13 Dreams*. W.W. Norton, 1977.

_____*Death and the Good Life*. St. Martin's Press, 1981.

_____*Death of the Kapowsin Tavern*. Harcourt, Brace, & World, 1965.

_____*Good Luck in Cracked Italian*. The World Publishing Co., 1969.

_____*The Lady in Kicking Horse Reservoir*. W.W. Norton, 1973.

_____*Making Certain It Goes On: The Collected Poems of Richard Hugo*. W.W. Norton, 1983.

_____*The Right Madness on Skye*. W.W. Norton, 1980.

_____*A Run of Jacks*. University of Minnesota Press, 1961.

_____*Sea Lanes Out*. Dooryard Press, 1983.

_____*Selected Poems*. W.W. Norton, 1979.

_____*The Triggering Town*. W.W. Norton, 1979.

_____*What Thou Lovest Well Remains American*. W.W. Norton, 1975.

_____*White Center*. W.W. Norton, 1980.

Jaeger, Lowell. *The Banana Man*. Pudding House Press, 2006.

_____ *Black Ice*. Pudding House Press, 2006.

_____*Greatest Hits*. Pudding House Press, 2000.

_____*Hope Against Hope*. Utah State University Press, 1990.

_____*Law of the Fish*. Wright Impressions, 1989.

_____*Native Land*. Pudding House Press, 1985.

_____*Nobody Special*. Pudding House Press, 2006.

_____*Nothing Lasts Forever*. Wright Impressions, 1990.

_____*Star-Crossed*. Pudding House Press, 2006.

_____*War on War*. Utah State University Press, 1987.

Jelinski, Jack. *Water Like the Soul of an Angel*. Howling Loon Press, 2005.

Keeler, Greg. *American Falls*. Confluence Press, 1987.

_____*Epiphany at Goofy's Gas*. Clark City Press 1992.

_____*The Far Bank*. Confluence Press, 1985.

_____*A Mirror to the Safe*. Limberlost Press, 1997.

_____*Sea Widow's Journal: To a Fisherman Drowned*. Tapir Press, 2000.

_____*Spring Catch*. Confluence Press, 1983.

_____*Waltzing With the Captain: Remembering Richard Brautigan*. Limberlost Press, 2004.

Klink, Joanna. *They are Sleeping*. University of Georgia Press, 2000.

_____*Circadian*. Penguin, 2007.

Kwasny, Melissa. *The Archival Birds*. Bear Star Press, 2000.

_____ *Modern Daughters and the Outlaw West*. Spinsters Ink, 1990.

_____*Reading Novalis in Montana*. Milkweed Editions, 2008.

_____*Thistle*. Lost Horse Press, 2006.

_____*Toward the Open Field: Poets on the Art of Poetry 1800-1950*. Wesleyan University Press, 2004.

_____*Trees Call for What They Need*. Spinsters Ink, 1994.

Lahey, Ed. *Apples Rolling on the Lawn*. Montana Writing Cooperative, 1999.

_____*Birds of a Feather*. Clark City Press, 2005.

_____*The Blind Horses*. Montana Arts Council, 1979.

_____*The Blind Horses and Still More Poems*. University of Montana, 2001.

_____*The Thin Air Gang*. Clark City Press, 2007.

Lee, Robert. *Guiding Elliott*. Lyons Press, 1997.

Lundy, Gary. *lavish is saying nothing like again*. blue malady press, 1997.

_____*this making i tore the sight from*. Sweetbrier Press, 1996.

_____ *to each other water cool and pure*. blue malady press, 2003.

Malo, Eve. *Dynamite Women: The Ten Women Nobel Peace Laureates of the 20ᵗʰ Century*. Vantage Press, 2009.

_____*Kindergarten Handbook: Self Concept Through Developmentally Appropriate Practice*. Montana Department of Education, 1991. (with J. Bullard)

McRae, Wally. *Cowboy Curmudgeon*. Gibb Smith, Publisher, 1992.

_____ *It's Just Grass and Water*. Oxalis Group, 1986.

_____*Things of Intrinsic Worth*. Outlaw Books, 1989.

_____*Up North Is Down The Crick*. Museum of the Rockies, 1985.

Nealon, M.J. *Immaculate Fuel.* Four Way Books, 2004.

———*Rogue Apostle.* Four Way Books, 2000.

Newby, Rick. *The Man in the Green Loden Overcoat.* Second Story Verlag, 1983.

———*Old Friends Walking in the Mountains: Poems.* Bedrock Editions, 1994.

———*A Radiant Map of the World: Poems.* Arrow Graphics/Montana Arts Council, 1981.

———*Sketches Begun in My Studio on a Sunday Afternoon and Completed the Following Day Near the Noon Hour on the Lower Slopes of the Rocky Mountains.* Editions Koch, 2008.

———*The Suburb of Long Suffering: Poems and Prose.* Bedrock Editions, 2002.

Noethe, Sheryl. *The Descent of Heaven Over the Lake.* New Rivers Press, 1984.

———*Ghost Openings.* Grace Court Press, 2000.

———*Poetry Everywhere.* Teachers and Writers Collaborative, 2006.

Noonan, Ed. *Noisy Soil: Selected Works 1980-1998.* Bedrock Books, 1998.

———*Good St. Dominic's Cat: A Cat in Heaven.* Mary's Mountain Press, 2000.

Old Coyote, Elnora A. *Cheatgrass and Tumbleweed,* Fenske Companies, 2000.

Owens, Greg. *Home Front.* Broadway Play Publishing, 2006.

———*The Life and Times of Tulsa Lovechild.* Broadway Play Publishing, 2004.

Pack, Robert. *Affirming Limits: Essays on Mortality, Choice, and Poetic Form.* University of Massachusetts Press, 1985.

———*Belief and Uncertainty in the Poetry of Robert Frost.* New England University Press, 2003.

———*Clayfield Rejoices, Clayfield Laments: A Sequence of Poems.* David Godine Press, 1987.

———*Composing Voices: A Cycle of Dramatic Monologues.* Crazyhorse Press, 2005.

———*Elk in Winter.* Chicago University Press, 2004.

———*Faces in a Single Tree: A Cycle of Dramatic Monologues.* David Godine Press, 1984.

———*Fathering the Map: New and Selected Later Poems.* Chicago University Press, 1993.

———*Guarded by Women.* Random House, 1963.

———*Home From the Cemetery.* Rutgers University Press, 1969.

———*The Irony of Joy.* Scribners, 1955.

———*Keeping Watch.* Rutgers University Press, 1969.

———*The Long View: Essays on the Discipline and Hope of Poetic Craft.* University of Massachusetts Press, 1991.

———*Minding the Sun.* Chicago University Press, 1996.

———*Nothing But Light.* Rutgers University Press, 1973.

———*Rounding It Out.* Chicago University Press, 1999.

_____*Selected Poems.* London: Chatto and Windus, 1964.

_____*A Stranger's Privilege.* MacMillan, 1959.

_____*Waking to My Name: New and Selected Poems.* Johns Hopkins Press, 1980.

Pankowski, Elsie. *Gathering Stones.* Pudding House Press, 2003.

_____*Sunrust Featured Poet Chapbook.* Sunrust Magazine, 1989.

Pape, Greg. *American Flamingo.* Southern Illinois University Press, 2005.

_____*Black Branches.* Carnegie Mellon University Press, 2005.

_____*Border Crossings.* University of Pittsburgh Press, 1978.

_____*Little America.* The Maguey Press, 1976.

_____*The Morning Horse.* Confluence Press, 1991.

_____*Small Pleasures.* Langniappe Press, 1994.

_____*Storm Pattern.* University of Pittsburgh Press, 1992.

_____*Sunflower Facing the Sun.* University of Iowa Press, 1992.

Parks, Amy Ratto. *Bread and Water Body.* University of Montana, 2004.

Pinet, Carolyn. *Poesies.* Presses de Villejuif, 1998.

Real Bird, Henry. *Best of Hank Real Bird.* HRB Press.

_____*Beyond Reflection.* HRB Press.

_____*Reflections and Shadows.* HRB Press.

_____*Where Shadows Are Born.* HRB Press.

Ruble, Sheila. *Listening To Stones.* Pronghorn Press, 2004.

Schemm, Ripley. *Mapping My Father.* Dooryard Press, 1981.

_____*Writing for her Life: The Novelist Mildred Walker.* University of Nebraska Press, 2003.

Shimoda, Brandon. *Lake M: Book One.* Corollary Press, 2007.

Slicer, Deborah. *The White Calf Kicks.* Autumn House Press, 2003.

Smith, Marie. *An Aussie Turned Cowboy Wife.* Clearview Publications, 1987.

_____*Exchanging Courtesies.* Heritage Press, 2004.

_____*North and East Down Under.* Clearview Publications,1990.

Smoker, M.L. *Another Attempt At Rescue.* Hanging Loose Press, 2005.

Soular, Jim. *The Thousand Yard Stare.* AuthorHouse, 2004.

Swan, Mac. *Let There Be Lit! A Resource Guide for Teachers of Montana Literature*. Montana Committee For The Humanities, 1988.

Thomas, Dave. *Buck's Last Wreck*. Wild Variety Books, 1996.
_____*Fossil Fuel*. Montana Writing Cooperative, 1977.
_____*The Hellgate Wind*. Camphorweed Press, 2004.

Uda, Lowell. *Under the Hala Tree*. Prickly Pear Press, 1980.

Umphrey, Michael L. *The Breaking Edge*. University of Montana, 1988.
_____*The Lit Window*. Cleveland State University, 1987.

Volkman, Karen. Crash's Law. W.W. Norton, 1996.
_____*Nomina*. BOA Editions, 2009.
_____*Spar*. University of Iowa Press, 2002.

Welch, James. *The Death of Jim Loney*. Penguin, 1987.
_____*Fools Crow*. Penguin, 1987.
_____*The Heartsong of Charging Elk*. Doubleday, 2000.
_____*The Indian Lawyer*. Norton, 2007.
_____*Killing Custer*. Norton, 2007.
_____ *Riding The Earthboy 40*. Penguin, 2004.
_____*Winter in the Blood*. Penguin, 1986.

Zarzyski, Paul. *All This Way For The Short Ride*. The Museum of New Mexico Press, 1996.
_____*Becoming Flight*. Heavy Duty Press, 2004.
_____*Blue Collar Light*. Red Wing Press, 1998.
_____*Call Me Lucky*. Confluence Press, 1981.
_____*The Garnet Moon*. The Black Rock Press, 1990.
_____*I Am Not A Cowboy*. Dry Crik Press, 1995.
_____*The Make-Up of Ice*.University of Georgia Press, 1984.
_____*Roughstock Sonnets*. The Lowell Press, 1989.
_____*Tracks*. The Kutenai Press, 1989.
_____*Wolf Tracks On The Welcome Mat*. Oreana Books, 2003.

Publication of *Poems Across the Big Sky* has been made possible by the generosity of the following donors:

Montana Cultural Trust
Anonymous—San Francisco
Anonymous—Kalispell
Anonymous—Lakeside
Lowell and Amy Jaeger—Bigfork
Flathead Bank—Bigfork
Mark and Christa Nadeau—Kalispell
Robert M. O'Neil—Kalispell
Foxy Lady Boutique—Polson
Suit Your Fancy—Kalispell
Roger Dunsmore—Dillon
Eve Malo—Dillon
Three Rivers Bank (1) —Kalispell
Three Rivers Bank (2) —Kalispell
Little Bears—Bigfork
Jack Jelinski—Bozeman
Bill and Diane Yarus—Kalispell
Robin Hamilton—Missoula
Rick DeMarinis—Missoula
Greg Keeler—Bozeman
Judy Blunt—Missoula
Jeff and Chris Ferderer—Troy
June Safford—Bozeman
Ripley Schemm Hugo—Missoula
Margaret Kingsland—Missoula
JoAnn Troxel—Bozeman
J.D. Whitney—Wausau, WI
Alan Weltzien—Dillon
Kathy Reick—Butte
Dr. David Murdock—Kalispell
Tony Smith—Troy
Sid Gustafson—Bozeman Veterinary Clinic
Dr. Ed Wettach—Kalispell
Thurston Orthodontics—Kalispell
Elizabeth Wood—Roundup
Dr. Peter B. and Carol Nelson—Kalispell
Casey Charles—Missoula
Dr. William Ferril—Whitefish
Jim Deatherage—Kennewick, WA

Loren Graham—Helena
Dr. Douglas and Barbara Nelson—Kalispell
Dr. Steven Johnson—Kalispell
Melby's Home Interiors—Columbia Falls
Dr. Thomas Colyer—Kalispell
Maxwell Milton—Helena
Maddy Etter—Casa Español—Kalispell
Mac Swan—Polson
Joe Legate—Kalispell
John Holbrook—Missoula
David and Donna Dale—Big Arm
Minerva Allen—Dodson
Cass Still—Yellow Bay
Greg Pape—Stevensville
Mark Cheff—Arlee
David Caserio—Billings
Paul Zalis—Somers
Christopher and Carolyn Pinet—Bozeman
Kelly Weaver—Seeley Lake
Beth Ferris—Missoula
Elnora A. Old Coyote—Huntley
Danell Jones—Billings
Benjamin and Emily Steele—Billings
Madeline DeFrees—Seattle, WA
Thomas and Elsie Pankowski—Great Falls
Great Falls Writers Group
Wanda and Milton Rosseland—Circle
Lois Welch—Missoula
Sheila Ruble—Billings
Donna Davis—Billings
Wayne and Kathy Murray—Kalispell
Terry Neil—San Francisco
Alex Alviar—Missoula
Anna Nesbitt—Bothel, WA
John Haines—Missoula
Mary Beth Gloege—Billings
M.J. Nealon—Missoula
Tom Elliott—Livingston
Linda Swanberg—Missoula
Vicki Beebe—Missoula